MW00638505

CHANCELLORSVILLE:
CROSSROADS OF FIRE

by Chris Mackowski

Copyright © 2011 by Chris Mackowski
Printed and bound in the United States of America
Published by THOMAS PUBLICATIONS
P.O. Box 3031
Gettysburg, Pa. 17325

All rights reserved. No part of this book may be used or reproduced without
written permission of the author and the publisher, except in the case of
brief quotations embodied in critical essays and reviews.

ISBN 978-1-57747-165-3

Design and production by Jackson Foster, The I.D. Entity, Fredericksburg, Virginia

For PJV. Mr. Bad Example

ACKNOWLEDGEMENTS

Most importantly, I thank historian Kristopher D. White, whose work and support literally made this book possible. We spent many, many hours on the battlefield together, and it was always time well spent. I could not have written this book without him.

I appreciate the support of my colleagues at Fredericksburg & Spotsylvania National Military Park, especially John Hennessy, Greg Mertz, Don Pfanz, Janice Frye, and Noel Harrison, who all made contributions to this volume. Frank O'Reilly's maps of the wartime battlefield were invaluable. I offer special thanks to Eric Mink, whose editorial work on the book proved extremely useful.

At St. Bonaventure University's Russell J. Jandoli School of Journalism and Mass Communication, I thank Patrick Vecchio, John Hanchette, Mary Beth Garvin, and the dean, Lee Coppola.

My thanks go out to Heidi Hartley, Jennifer Doron McConnell, Lauren Ruffini, and Felix Was for proofreading help. Thanks, too, to John Cummings and the Friends of Fredericksburg Area Battlefields for their continued support of my writing projects. Designer Jackson Foster of The I.D. Entity continues to make my words pop on the page.

Finally, I am ever indebted to the support given to me by my family, especially Heidi and my children, Stephanie and Jackson.

CONTENTS

TOURING THE CHANCELLORSVILLE BATTLEFIELD

The same roads that brought the two armies into conflict around Chancellorsville in May of 1863 continue to serve a great many people. For battlefield visitors, those roads can both help and hinder a tour of the battlefield.

The organization of this book and tour reflects knowledge of those roads. It also takes into consideration related information such as park facilities and the availability of parking.

Therefore, for the sake of your safety, I'll talk about some events slightly out of sequence. (In such instances, I'll always be sure to let you know.)

Please keep in mind that Route 3 has two lanes of eastbound and two lanes of westbound traffic, and the roads are frequently busy. Please also note that some park roads are one way; others are not paved. All park roads and trails receive year-round maintenance.

What will the country say?

Oh, what will the country say?

—*President Abraham Lincoln following the Battle of Chancellorsville*

PROLOGUE: THE WOUNDING
OF STONEWALL JACKSON

On the night of May 2, 1863, Lieutenant General Thomas Jonathan "Stonewall" Jackson led his staff down the Mountain Road on a reconnaissance mission in front of the main Confederate line. The mission would end in calamity for the Confederates.

Night had set in, and the attack had faltered. The full moon rising above the treeline couldn't pierce the gloom of the Wilderness, thicker than even the impossibly thick foliage.

The Plank Road, which cut through the region, would have provided a clear, well-lit avenue for the reconnaissance party, but it would have also left them exposed to enemy fire. Instead, their guide, a nineteen-year-old named David Kyle, led them down a lesser-known path called the Mountain Road, which didn't show up on the maps. Kyle knew the road because he'd grown up in these parts—on the Bullock Farm, in fact, just a mile away. This was literally his back yard.

At the head of the party rode Confederate Lieutenant General Thomas Jonathan "Stonewall" Jackson. Leery of this uncharted territory, he told Kyle to lead the way, but the general was soon satisfied that Kyle wasn't leading them into a trap. He trotted his horse past Kyle's and continued down the Mountain Road, his seven staff members following closely.

Behind them lay the main Confederate battle line straddling the Plank Road and the Mountain Road. Ahead of the riders, somewhere in the gloom, the 33rd North Carolina Infantry stood vigil as pickets. Jackson and his staff rode a couple hundred yards down the Mountain Road—not quite reaching the picket line—and they stopped.

And Jackson listened.

The Bullock Road branched away from the Orange Turnpike and ran to the northeast, where it passed the Bullock Farm and intersected with Ely's Ford Road. On the night of May 2, Confederates organized their line along the road.

For the past four hours, Jackson and the twenty-eight thousand Confederates under his command had been pushing the Union army back through these woods after a surprise attack on the unprotected Union right flank. Jackson had led his entire Second Corps on an all-day march through the Wilderness of Spotsylvania County to get into position. When he launched the attack at 5:15 in the afternoon, he caught most of the Union army off guard. While the Confederates did face some resistance, Jackson pressed the attack forward as aggressively as possible until nightfall and the Wilderness itself sapped away Confederate momentum.

Jackson wasn't ready to quit, though. He wanted to give his men the chance to regroup and give reinforcements the chance to move up—and then he wanted to renew the advance.

As he sat on his horse, under the dark canopy of trees along the Mountain Road, listening through the forest, the sounds he heard confirmed his fears: chopping, digging, shoveling. Union soldiers, only a few hundreds yards ahead, were building entrenchments to resist the next Confederate attack.

And attack he must. He had to reunite his half of the army with the half commanded by General Robert E. Lee, still on

Returning from his reconnaissance mission, Jackson and his staff were accidentally caught in a wave of musket fire that had rippled up the Confederate line from the south.

the far side of the battlefield. The Union army, trapped between the Confederate wings, was vulnerable—but likewise, the Confederate army, separated as it was, was also vulnerable.

Jackson could wait until morning, but then his men would have to storm positions the Union army would have spent all night fortifying. Or, he could launch a risky night attack now while the Union army was still off balance.

He liked his chances now.

Jackson turned his horse back toward the main Confederate line.

And then the night erupted in fire.

★ ★ ★ ★ ★

Earlier in the evening, as the Confederate advance had swept forward, a regiment of Union cavalry, the 8th Pennsylvania, suddenly burst from the woods along the Plank Road. Finding themselves trapped between the Confederate skirmish line and the main battle line, their commander ordered, "Draw sabers and charge!" They wheeled toward the east in an attempt to break out but were repulsed. They reversed direction and tried to charge the main battle line but again

Brigadier General James Lane, commander of the men who accidentally shot Jackson.

met a withering volley. The survivors scattered into the woods on both sides of the road and were able to make their way back to Union lines, leaving behind thirty-three casualties and a pile of eighty dead horses.

A short time later, to the south of the Plank Road, a regiment of Pennsylvania infantry, lost in the woods as dark was setting in, slipped in unseen between the Confederate picket line and the main battle line. After brushing up against a regiment of North Carolinians, the Pennsylvanians tried to talk their way out of their predicament, but to no avail. They went rearward as captives—along with rumors of Yankees wandering around out in the darkness.

First enemy cavalry, now enemy infantry. Enemies, it seemed, lurked everywhere. "No one could tell friend from foe nor see a hidden enemy a rod away," a Union officer said.

Still charged with adrenaline from their attack, but with nowhere to go once their advance had halted, Confederates seemed especially jumpy. Individual soldiers fired at shadows, at strange sounds, at phantom enemies. At the south end of the line, skittish Confederates fired into the brush, spooking the men to their left, who likewise fired into the brush. The series of shots picked up momentum and sizzled up the Confederate line like a firecracker fuse.

Just as Jackson and his men were returning from their reconnaissance, the Confederate fire rolled across Jackson's front, catching Jackson and his men.

"Stop!" cried one of Jackson's staff officers, whose horse had been shot out from beneath him. "You're firing into your own men!"

"It's a lie!" came the response from the veteran North Carolinians posted along the Confederate battle line. "Pour it into them, boys!"

One of Jackson's staff members fell dead, another wounded. Three bullets struck Jackson. One of the wounds, in the right hand, would prove relatively minor. The other two wounds, in the left arm, would prove much more serious.

Along the Plank Road, one of Jackson's subordinates, Major General Ambrose Powell "A. P." Hill, had been leading

a reconnaissance party of his own. His staff, caught in the rolling thunder that swept up the line, suffered far more grievously than Jackson's. Of the nine men with him, only Hill remained unscathed: The others lay dead or wounded or had their horses bolt eastward into enemy lines.

Jackson's staff evacuated the general from the field only with difficulty. The sounds of the Confederate muskets had alerted Federal artillerymen to their presence, and soon the cannoneers opened fire on the Confederate position.

Hill, who took command following Jackson's accident, was injured by one of these artillery blasts. Jackson's other two division commanders, generals Robert Rodes and Raleigh E. Colston, were both too inexperienced to lead the entire Second Corps, so Hill sent for Confederate cavalry commander Jeb Stuart to take charge.

It would be hours before Stuart could arrive on the field, though. When he finally did, he inherited a situation he knew almost nothing about. The man best suited to brief him, Stonewall Jackson, was out of the action—under the surgeon's knife, having his left arm amputated at a field hospital several miles to the rear.

Despite the light of the full moon, Jackson and his staff had been shrouded in darkness because of the thick foliage crowding in along the edge of the Mountain Road, which made it impossible for Confederates along the main battle line to see them.

Members of Jackson's staff eased the general from his panicked horse and tried to gauge the severity of his wounds.

Thus ended the fighting on May 2, 1863. The Confederate army sat dangerously divided and with part of its leadership in disarray. The Union army, rocked back on its heels but not defeated, had time to regroup.

The battle of Chancellorsville was far from over.

In fact, the most serious fighting had not even begun.

At the Visitor Center

CHRONOLOGICALLY, JACKSON'S WOUNDING TAKES PLACE between tour stops 10 and 11.

Visitors today can have a difficult time understanding the story of Jackson's wounding because the landscape around the visitor center has changed so dramatically since 1863. The visitor center itself, constructed in 1963, obliterated much of the old Mountain Road trace, which ran right through the building's current location. For years, the National Park Service's philosophy dictated that visitor services be located as close to the battlefield's most important action as possible. From a preservation standpoint, of course, that philosophy proved highly disruptive, and current practices now steer away from such intrusive placement.

The old Mountain Road bisects the spot now occupied by the Chancellorsville Battlefield Visitor Center.

Fortunately, an original section of the Mountain Road still exists. In 2007, the park restored part of the road trace. From the northeast corner of the building, a walk of less than a hundred feet will take visitors down to the Mountain Road. A sign at the far end of the road marks the approximate location of Jackson's farthest advance. It was there that he stopped to listen to the Union soldiers as they worked. The Confederate picket line, also ahead of him through the forest, would have been located approximately where the eastern entrance into the parking lot turns in from Route 3.

While the Mountain Road now looks much as it did in 1863, much else is different. Most importantly, the forest has matured. The trees today are much larger than they would've been in 1863. This entire section of Virginia—seventy square miles of it—was known as the Wilderness because of the dense second-growth forest that grew here. The forests had previously been clear-cut to support the local iron ore industry, but by the spring of 1863, a second-growth forest had sprung up. The foliage was shorter and denser than it is now, packed with clinging vines, prickly thorns, scrubby brush, and whip-like saplings—all of it thick and lush and fighting for light. It was, as one officer described it, "a wilderness in the most forbidding sense of the word."

It's difficult, in the open glen to the north of the visitor center, with the cathedral of trees that offers so much visibility, to visualize what that Wilderness looked like. The National

The Mountain Road today.

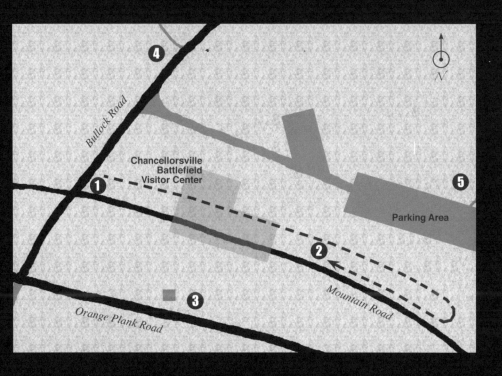

As the Confederate advance bogged down in the thick Wilderness, their foremost units reformed in a line of battle along the Bullock Road. Second Corps commander "Stonewall" Jackson and his staff rode beyond the Confederate line on a reconnaissance mission along the Mountain Road (1). However, Jackson and his men did not go beyond the Confederate picket line; instead, after stopping and listening, they turned around to return to the main Confederate line. Less than one hundred yards from safety, Jackson's party was caught by a wave of friendly fire (2). Today, a pair of monuments marks the general area where the incident took place (3), but they don't mark the exact location because the people who placed the monuments wanted them visible from the road. The west loop of the Chancellorsville History Trail (4) and the east loop of the trail (5) both provide insights into the terrain the armies had to fight through.

Park Service does maintain a small patch of second-growth foliage, located between the west side of the visitor center and the Bullock Road, to give visitors at least a sense of the Wilderness's density, although even this patch is only about half as thick as it would have been in 1863.

Tucked behind the visitor center, almost along the edge of Route 3, stands a monument to Jackson. Dedicated in 1888, the monument was placed in its present location to mark the area—although not the exact spot—where Jackson was wounded. At the time, some disagreement arose about the exact location of Jackson's wounding, but in the end, pragmatism won out: The monument committee wanted the granite structure close to the road so that passers-by could see it. (Ironically, a hedgerow now hides the monument from travelers.) Twenty feet away, a quartz boulder, placed there prior to the monument's construction, served as the area's first marker.

Bullock Road, which runs along the west edge of the parking lot and leads to Tour Stop 1, did exist at the time of the battle. A pair of North Carolina regiments—including the 18th

The open lawn and tall trees around the battlefield visitor center belie the true nature of the Wilderness, which looked more like the area of tangled, thorny scrub brush located between the lawn and Bullock Road.

This post-war photo of the Orange Plank Road shows how exposed the road was. On the left sits the quartz boulder placed along the roadside sometime between 1876 and 1885 to mark the area where Jackson was shot.

North Carolina, the unit that accidentally shot Jackson—lined up along the far side of the road; the main Confederate battle line also stretched through the woods on the south side of the Plank Road (modern Route 3), although the road that's there today, Stuart Drive, did not exist at the time of the battle.

On the far side of Bullock Road, the western loop of the Chancellorsville History Trail, which is only 0.6 miles, winds through the forest toward a set of Union trenches. The trenches were constructed by the Union Third Corps but were abandoned when the corps moved south toward Catharine Furnace late on the morning of May 2 (you'll read about that in Chapter 8). Had the Third Corps remained in this vicinity and been manning those trenches when the Confederate flank attack swept through this area, they might have been able to blunt the effects of Jackson's attack.

The eastern loop of the Chancellorsville History Trail leaves from the visitor center parking lot near the picnic area. The trail, which is clearly marked and well maintained, runs through a dense patch of forest for about 0.8 miles before coming out in a clearing near the ruins of the Chancellor House. The walk offers a fairly good glimpse of the kind of forest soldiers from both sides were trying to fight through.

▶▶ TO STOP 1:

Exit the parking lot by taking a right onto Bullock Road. Follow Bullock Road 0.7 miles to the former site of the Bullock Farm. Pull over in the parking area on the right side of the road.

CHAPTER ONE

THE ROAD TO CHANCELLORSVILLE

Sixty thousand Union soldiers converged on Chancellorsville from U.S. Ford, Ely's Ford and Germanna Ford.

They filed into the Wilderness in long blue lines, marching four abreast, sixty thousand in all. They flowed over the Rapidan and Rappahannock Rivers from the north, across U.S. Ford, Ely's Ford, and farthest to the west, Germanna Ford.

The army's morale was higher than it had been in months. Following the catastrophe in Fredericksburg the previous December, when it had suffered some thirteen thousand casualties in a series of vain attacks against fortified Confederate positions, and then the humiliation of the "Mud March" in January when its attempt to flank the Confederate army bogged down in soupy roads and terrible weather, the army's morale had sunk to near-despair.

That had all changed, though, when President Lincoln promoted Major General Joseph Hooker to the command of the Army of the Potomac.

"I have heard, in such a way as to believe it, of your recently saying that the Army and the Government needed a Dictator," Lincoln wrote to Hooker when making the appointment. "Of course it was not for this, but in spite of it, that I have given you command. Only those generals who gain successes, can set up dictators. What I now ask of you is military success, and I will risk the dictatorship."

Lincoln pointed out that there were things about Hooker he was "not quite satisfied with," but he also offered his new commander praise: "I believe you to be a brave and skillful soldier, which, of course, I like…. You have confidence in

Ely's Ford Road.

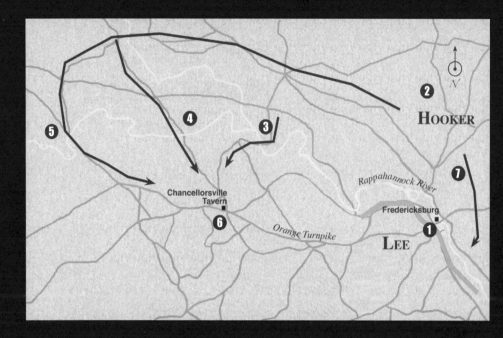

Following the Battle of Fredericksburg in December 1862, the Confederate army had spent the winter in the heights to the west of the city (1) while the Union army spent the winter across the Rappahannock River in Falmouth (2). Union Major General Joseph Hooker opened the spring campaign by marching the bulk of his army on a wide sweeping movement around the Confederates, crossing at U.S. (3), Ely's (4), and Germanna (5) fords, with the objective of converging on the Chancellorsville intersection (6). Meanwhile, a portion of the Union army stayed behind (7) to serve as a decoy while the rest of the army advanced on Lee's rear. Lee would learn of Hooker's plan, though, and move west along the Orange Turnpike to intercept the Federals.

yourself, which is a valuable, if not an indispensable, quality. You are ambitious, which, within reasonable bounds, does more good than harm."

Union Major General Joseph "Fighting Joe" Hooker (center, with the black hat) and his staff.

Hooker had earned a reputation as a hard fighter— a reputation cemented by a nickname to match when a newspaper headline accidentally omitted a dash from a correspondent's report: "Fighting—Joe Hooker." The misprint ran as "Fighting Joe Hooker," and the nickname stuck. Hooker himself disliked the moniker because he thought it made him sound too rash, but his men loved it.

Following his promotion to commanding general, Hooker's first order of business had been to reorganize the army and rebuild morale. As soon as Hooker assumed command, fresh supplies began to roll into the army's camps in Stafford County, Virginia, on the north side of the Rappahannock. Hooker had bake ovens installed, and soon the men had fresh bread four days a week. Some camps received oysters and champagne. Men were given furloughs to go home and visit loved ones. Morale soared—and so did the confidence the fighting men had in Fighting Joe Hooker.

By spring, Hooker had devised a plan to engage the Confederate Army, which still sat in its winter camps on the far side of the Rappahannock River in the heights beyond

Joe Hooker instilled a renewed sense of morale in the Army of the Potomac. In early April, the army showed off its pride to President Lincoln in a series of grand reviews.

Fredericksburg. Hooker would leave a portion of his army behind as a decoy to keep the Confederates in place while the bulk of his force marched north and west and then swung down around behind the unsuspecting Confederates, either trapping them against the river in Fredericksburg or forcing them to retreat toward Richmond and out into the open. Hooker's cavalry, meanwhile, would slip to the south of the Confederate Army and disrupt their lines of communication and supply, which would leave Confederate General Robert E. Lee no choice but to engage in battle.

"My plans are perfect," Hooker declared, "and when I carry them out, may God have mercy on General Lee, for I will have none."

And so on Tuesday, April 27, 1863, Hooker began a long, circuitous march to outflank the Confederates. Forty-two thousand men slipped quietly out of their camps, leaving behind twenty-five thousand men as decoys. To add to the ruse, Hooker sent another forty thousand men across the Rappahannock south of Fredericksburg. Those men, under the command of Major General John Sedgwick, had the job of holding the Confederate Army's attention while Hooker led the bulk of the army on its northwesterly sweep.

Hooker's plan resembled the one Major General Ambrose Burnside had tried to execute in January—the ill-fated Mud March that proved to be Burnside's undoing. The weather notwithstanding, the plan itself had been sound—sound enough that Hooker, when he carried it out, met with surprising success in the earliest stages of his march. The plan depended on speed and secrecy, which Hooker achieved. His men moved some forty miles in three days, splitting into three separate columns to avoid congestion.

Union forces march into the Wilderness.

The soldiers, glad to again be on the move after months in camp, and ready to redeem that dreadful loss in December, marched with high spirits they sang:

"The Union boys are moving on the left and on the right,
The bugle-call is sounding; our shelters we must strike;
Joe Hooker is our leader, he takes his whiskey strong,
So our knapsacks we will sling, and go marching along."

On April 30, lead elements of Hooker's army crossed at Ely's Ford. A Confederate brigade, guarding the approach from the ford, tried to delay the Union advance. "My men were very anxious indeed to fire at them," wrote Lieutenant Colonel Everand M. Feild, commanding the 12th Virginia Infantry.

Feild deployed his men near the Bullock Farm and waited for the northerners to approach. "[T]he enemy [soon]…came forward from the woods on the opposite side of the field with a heavy force of cavalry, and moved down on us," Feild said. When the Union skirmishers advanced to within about 250 yards, Feild gave the order for his Virginians to fire. "[A]nd of the 250 muskets not a single one fired," Feild said. Rain had fouled the muskets. "The strain of that moment was the most severe that I had during the war," he admitted.

Federals advanced as the Confederates hurriedly cleaned and reloaded, getting off enough scattered shots to stop the advance long enough for Feild's men to escape.

Hooker's army moved onward.

The Bullock Farm

① TOUR STOP

WITH SO MUCH CONSTRUCTION AND DEVELOPMENT IN THE area today, it's hard to imagine that the Wilderness was once one of the most rugged parts of Virginia. Despite its name, though, the Wilderness was not entirely wild. A number of small farms, such as the one located here, owned by Oscar Bullock, had been cut out of the rough second-growth jungle.

Bullock owned 300 acres in the Wilderness of Spotsylvania County. On this property, he constructed a modest two-and-a-half story home where he lived with his wife, Catharine, their two children, Thomas and Jessie, and Catharine's brother, David Kyle. The Bullocks owned five slaves, who lived in a nearby cabin. When the battle of Chancellorsville erupted, Bullock was serving in the 30th Virginia Infantry, Kyle was serving in the 9th Virginia Cavalry, and Catharine and the children remained in the home.

On May 3, after sustaining an injury during battle, Hooker moved his headquarters to the Bullock House, a mile to the north of the Chancellorsville intersection.

After the collapse of the Federal position around Chancellorsville, Hooker established a new line, its flanks securely anchored on the Rapidan River and its apex across the road from the Bullock Farm.

Imagine standing on the porch of your farmhouse as a massive column of soldiers swept by. They came from Ely's Ford, up the road to the left, and marched down what is now modern state Route 610 toward Chancellorsville, an intersection another six-tenths of a mile to the right.

On the night of April 30, after the army had halted its march for the day, soldiers from the Union Second Corps bivouacked on this property.

On May 1, Federals set up a field hospital in the house. "[O]perating tables were improvised by detaching some of the doors from their hinges, with the addition of a few boards found about the premises," wrote the Third Corps's medical director. When the house came under Confederate fire, the surgeons moved their hospital closer to the ford.

On May 3, the Union Army passed this way again as it fell back from the Chancellorsville intersection—some of the men demoralized by defeat, others enraged although impotent to do anything about it. Hooker set up his headquarters next to the Bullock House, then moved inside the newly constructed fortifications built by his men on the far side of the road. Remnants of those protective earthworks still remain, and the hiking path across the road follows a stretch of that Federal line.

The presence of the armies meant ruin for the Bullocks. "[M]y home was entirely destroyed," Catharine wrote a few months after the battle. "The house torn down from necessity. Entrenchments cut all over the place. My servants all gone to the Yankees. I am now left without any support but the labor of my own hand."

▶▶ **TO STOP 2**

At the stop sign where Bullock Road meets Route 610, turn right. Proceed 0.5 miles. Just before you reach the traffic light at the intersection with Route 3, you will see a parking area on the right. Pull into the parking area. A small walking path at the south end of the parking lot will take you to the ruins of the Chancellor house.

Genl Hooker's Head Qurtrs at the Chancell
May 1st 1863. Edwin F.

CHAPTER TWO

THE MOST IMPORTANT CROSSROADS IN AMERICA

By April 30, 1863, Chancellorsville had become the most important intersection in the country.

As the columns of Union soldiers curled south, they aimed toward the crossroads of Chancellorsville, a tavern that sat at the intersection of Ely's Ford Road and the Orange Turnpike, some ten miles west of Fredericksburg. The two-story brick mansion, built in the early 1800s, had served for decades as a tavern and inn, but by the spring of 1863, with traffic on the roads only a fraction of what it used to be, the house served primarily as a private residence for Frances Chancellor and her six daughters.

Spearheading the movement down Ely's Ford Road, past the Bullock House, marched the men of Major General George Gordon Meade's Fifth Corps. "Four ladies in light, attractive spring costumes" came out of the Chancellor house to scold the men as they marched by, one Union soldier wrote. "[T]hey were not at all abashed or intimidated…. [They] scolded audibly and reviled bitterly."

Meade himself arrived at Chancellorsville on the afternoon of April 30, joined soon after by Major General Henry Slocum, who had crossed with his Twelfth Corps at Germanna Ford to the northwest and now marched toward the crossroads along the Orange Turnpike. "This is splendid, Slocum," Meade said to his colleague, still eyeing the path eastward. "Hurrah for old Joe! We are on Lee's flank, and he does not know it."

Union Twelfth Corps commander Major General Henry Slocum.

On the evening of April 30, Hooker sent a message to his men, expressing his "heartfelt satisfaction" at their progress thus far.

But just then, Hooker called off the advance. He wanted to give the army time to concentrate. Meade, in a letter to his wife that evening, expressed his disappointment: "We are across the river and have out-maneuvered the enemy, but we are not yet out of the woods."

Meade spoke both figuratively and literally. Fredericksburg still lay twelve miles away. Hooker, however, felt no need to hurry. He had the Confederates right where he wanted them. "The rebel army is now the legitimate property of the Army of the Potomac," he said.

Hooker sent a message to his men congratulating them on their success thus far: "It is with heartfelt satisfaction the commanding general announces to the army that the operations of the last three days have determined that our enemy must ingloriously fly, or come out from behind his defenses and give us battle on our own ground, where certain destruction awaits him."

The Chancellor House

TOUR STOP

DESPITE ITS NAME, CHANCELLORSVILLE WAS NOTHING more than a large brick home, sometimes used as a tavern and inn, built at an important crossroads that met in the eastern half of the Wilderness.

The remaining foundation shows the outline of the house, which was actually built in phases. Construction began on the original section of the house in 1813. By 1816, the Chancellorsville Tavern, "large and commodius for the entertainment of travellers," provided food and lodging for wayfarers heading up and down Ely's Ford Road and the newly constructed Turnpike that ran toward Fredericksburg. In addition, the building later housed a post office. By 1835, a new wing, two-and-a-half stories tall, was built, and after that, a storage area was added.

The Chancellor mansion proved to be a popular wayside for travelers passing through the Wilderness.

The same roads that brought the armies to Chancellorsville have become even busier in modern times as the population in Virginia has boomed.

The gravesite of the Rowley infants.

The first owners of the house, George and Ann Chancellor, had originally lived across the road at Fairview. Following George's death in 1836, the big brick house eventually moved out of the family's possession, changing hands at least twice. However, by 1863, Chancellors had again reoccupied the house, this time as renters, and Frances Chancellor and her six unmarried daughters had opened the inn for business.

In the early years of the war, Confederate soldiers stationed in the area frequented the inn, as much for the company of the young ladies as for the food. "My sisters were very nice to these defenders of our country, and played the piano and sang for them, and they taught my sisters to play cards, which my mother disapproved, but they all seemed to have a good time," recalled the youngest sister, Sue Chancellor, who was fourteen at the time.

When the enemy made raids into the area, the family's demeanor changed, Sue said. "My sisters were cold and distant," she recalled. "My mother had her whole crop of corn shelled and put into under-beds in the bedrooms of the house, and all of her stock of meat was hidden under the stone steps at the front door. There were several of these steps and the top one was lifted and the whole stock of hams, shoulders, and middling packed in the space underneath and the top stone replaced." The remains of those stone stairs still sit in front of the home's ruins.

Also of note at the Chancellor house site is the grave of two infants, a boy and a girl, both nameless, both of whom died in childbirth. Their parents, James and Etta Rowley, moved to Virginia from Texas in 1910 when their family purchased Chancellorsville and the adjacent 1,155 acres. A grape arbor had once been located next to the gravesite.

When the Union Army came to Chancellorsville, the Chancellor family hid valuables, including their meat, under the front steps of their home.

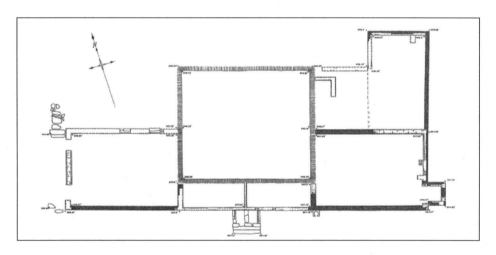

▶▶ TO STOP 3:

On May 3, the Chancellor house sat at the center of battle. You will return to this stop at the end of the tour for a closer look at how the military situation unfolded that day.

Exit the parking area and turn right. At the stoplight, turn left. Travel 2.5 miles. You will see a sign that indicates a left turn for a Civil War Trails marker. First pull into the median-crossing lane, then cross the westbound lane of Route 3 to the parking lot for the First Day at Chancellorsville Battlefield, where the action on May 1 took place. Be cautious of oncoming traffic.

Floorplan of the Chancellor House showing the original section of the house, the two wings that were later added, and the final rooms added to the rear.

Advance of Genl Sykes (regulars) May 1st

CHAPTER THREE

THE FIRST DAY'S BATTLE

Elements of the Union Fifth Corps moved eastward from Chancellorsville along the Orange Turnpike. (Image courtesy Library of Congress)

As smoothly as Hooker's plan had unfolded, his army hadn't marched all the way into the heart of the Wilderness unseen—or even unopposed. Confederate cavalry under Jeb Stuart had skirmished with the advancing Union troops as early as April 28. Stuart found it tough to gather dependable intelligence on Hooker's exact movements, though, so the information he sent back to Lee offered only a vague picture.

"I owe Mr. F. J. Hooker no thanks for keeping me here in this state of expectancy," Lee wrote in a letter to his wife. He referred to Hooker, with a mixture of scorn and amusement, by the nom-de-guerre the press had given the Union general: "Mr. F. J." stood for Mr. Fighting Joe.

Because Virginia provided Lee with a home-field advantage, Confederate sympathizers sent a stream of information in Lee's direction, augmenting Stuart's intelligence. Lee learned enough to grow worried. To better gauge the threat and protect his rear, Lee sent Richard Anderson's division, some 8,500 men, westward to watch the fords across the Rappahannock. Ordered by Lee to choose "the strongest line you can," Anderson deployed his troops along a north-south ridgeline that cut across the Orange Turnpike. A small stream, Mott's Run, ran parallel to the ridge. Just to the Confederate rear, along the south roadside, sat the Zoan Baptist Church.

Dig in, Anderson told his men. The Union juggernaut was coming.

* * * * *

**Confederate Major General
Richard Anderson.**

Even as Anderson settled into position, Lee put the rest of the Confederate army into motion. "[T]he main attack would come on our flank and rear," Lee had realized.

Lee decided to leave ten thousand soldiers under General Jubal Early to hold the Fredericksburg position and serve as a decoy to convince the Union First and Sixth Corps, who were themselves stationed along the Rappahannock as decoys, that the Confederates still manned the positions they had occupied since December.

Lee's plan violated all conventional military wisdom, which dictated that a commander never divide his forces in the face of a superior foe. Lee's numbers were already diminished because of the absence of Lieutenant General James Longstreet, detached with eighteen thousand troops to southeast Virginia to forage for the army and combat a Union presence in that region. Now Lee would divide his army once again by leaving Early's men in Fredericksburg while the rest of the Army of Northern Virginia—forty-five thousand men—turned its attention to "Mr. F. J. Hooker."

That gave Lee a total of fifty-five thousand men, including Early's detachment, to bring into the fight against Hooker's one-hundred-twenty thousand men. Lee knew he was sorely outnumbered, but he didn't necessarily consider himself outmatched. He could use the wooded terrain of the Wilderness around Chancellorsville to entangle Hooker's larger force. He also had the element of surprise on his side because Hooker still thought the Confederates remained hunkered down in Fredericksburg. Lee believed that if he hit strongly enough, he could do much to even the odds and allow himself, not Hooker, to set the tone of battle.

* * * * *

Shortly before dawn on Friday, May 1, Major General Lafayette McLaws arrived with 7,600 Confederate reinforcements to bolster Anderson's line. "It must be victory or death, for defeat would be ruinous," Lee had told them.

Then, around 8:00 a.m., Stonewall Jackson arrived on the field to take overall command. Lee had ordered his lieutenant

**Confederate commander
General Robert E. Lee.**

to "make arrangements to repulse the enemy." Jackson, ever offensive-minded, planned to repulse the enemy by slamming them head-on.

Jackson directed McLaws to move directly west out the turnpike toward Chancellorsville, and he directed Anderson to move in the same direction following the Orange Plank Road, which branched off the turnpike and ran roughly parallel to it to the south. As reinforcements from the Second Corps arrived on the field from Fredericksburg, Jackson told them, they would reinforce Anderson and McLaws as necessary. It would be, wrote one Confederate, "a supreme effort, a union of audacity & desperation."

By the time the Confederate advance got under way around 11:00 a.m., Joe Hooker had decided that he, too, was ready for action. He ordered George Meade to advance his Fifth Corps toward Fredericksburg along the River Road, which swept northeastward away from the turnpike before arcing back toward it near Banks' Ford, a key river crossing close to Fredericksburg. But of course, neither Meade nor Hooker realized that the Confederate army had redeployed

LEE'S PLAN VIOLATED
ALL CONVENTIONAL
MILITARY WISDOM,
WHICH DICTATED
THAT A COMMANDER
NEVER DIVIDE HIS
FORCES IN THE FACE
OF A SUPERIOR FOE.

Aggressive Confederate attacks couldn't compensate for superior Federal numbers.

and now waited for them on the edge of the Wilderness. Meade's main route of advance would, unbeknownst to him, put him in the vulnerable Confederate rear.

Meanwhile, another of Meade's divisions moved east straight down the turnpike. Along the Orange Plank Road to the south, the Twelfth Corps under Slocum also moved east.

The blue and gray columns, advancing in opposite directions on the same roads, clashed at twenty minutes past eleven.

"The fighting was hot and close [due to] the thick underbrush," said one Confederate. The two armies pushed at each other, but Jackson's aggressive nature couldn't compensate for the superior numbers of the Union Army, which fought well and began gaining ground. Confederates soon found themselves back near the fortifications they'd dug along the ridge by Mott's Run.

And then Hooker suddenly, inexplicably, called it off.

* * * * *

Later, after he had fallen from grace, Hooker tried to explain his decision. "I lost faith in Joe Hooker," he said.

The Confederate presence to his immediate east had caught the Union commander completely off guard. The Confederates, after all, were supposed to be twelve miles away in Fredericksburg. If his intelligence had been wrong concerning his opponents' location, what else might be wrong?

It didn't matter that his subordinates were adapting effectively to the new situation. It didn't matter that his army was pushing the enemy back. It didn't matter that Meade had

made it almost all the way to Banks' Ford virtually unopposed —which would have put him in a position to drop down behind the Confederate army and wreak havoc.

Hooker himself could not adapt to the changing circumstances. He folded under the pressure. "I was hazarding too much to continue the movement," he later said.

Hooker instead opted to pull his army back into a concentrated position around Chancellorsville. The orders made little sense to any of the Union commanders. "In no event should we give up our ground," one of them said.

But give it up they did. Hooker confirmed the order, and the army pulled back.

"The men went back disappointed, not without grumbling," said Brigadier General Alpheus Williams, "and it really required some policy to satisfy them that there was not mismanagement somewhere."

"The advance was stopped," another officer later wrote. "The battle of Chancellorsville was lost right there."

Hooker saw it differently. "It's all right…" he said to one of his corps commanders. "I have got Lee just where I want him. He must fight me on my own ground."

Just as Federals began to gain ground in their battle along the Orange Turnpike, Hooker ordered his army to disengage and concentrate back near Chancellorsville.

TOUR STOP ③

The First Day at Chancellorsville Battlefield

A walking trail gives visitors the chance to explore part of the First Day battlefield.

THE FIELDS ON EITHER SIDE OF MOTT'S RUN—TODAY known as Lick Run—provided the first real open space on the eastern edge of the Wilderness. For the Federals, getting into the open would allow them to deploy their vastly superior forces in powerful attack formations and bring their full weight to bear against the Confederates. Conversely, staying bottled up in the Wilderness would negate their numerical advantage by making it difficult to maneuver.

For the Confederates, the open space provided clear fields of fire. They could simply hunker down in their defensive works and await the Federal advance uphill across open ground. Those Confederate fortifications ran along the crest of a hill to the east of your current position, toward Fredericksburg, beyond the white-roofed barn. Zoan Church sat along that same crest on the south side of the road; the modern-day Zoan Church sits there today.

But Stonewall Jackson arrived, discontent to wait for the Union army to attack the fortified Confederate position. Taking the offensive, he sent half of the Confederates down the road you just drove in on and the other half down the Orange Plank Road, which ran roughly parallel to the south.

Later in the day, when the Federal army pushed the Confederates back, the Southerners grudgingly gave ground across these same fields. They finished the fight nearly where they'd begun it—but then Hooker recalled his army. The Federals had finally succeeded in reaching their goal—the open space beyond the Wilderness—when suddenly they had to let it slip away.

The Second Battle of Chancellorsville, waged over this very same ground, opened on July 31, 2002. A coalition of seven preservation groups announced its opposition to a planned eight-hundred-acre development known as

"The Town of Chancellorsville" that would include 1,995 homes and up to 2.2 million square feet of business space—all situated on property immediately adjacent to the National Park. In addition, a long-range transportation plan for the region called for a highway connector from Route 3 to I-95 that would cut across part of the battlefield.

In March 2003, after intense lobbying by preservation groups and local citizens, and a national petition drive that netted some 30,000 signatures, the county board of supervisors declined to approve the zoning changes that would make the development possible. Several months later, the proposed connector to I-95 was dropped from the long-range transportation plan.

In 2004, the Civil War Preservation Trust, a national battlefield preservation organization, bought 140 acres of the property, but another five hundred acres got sold to a developer who planned to build luxury homes. The developer offered to sell another 75 acres of historically significant land to the preservation group at a "substantially below-market price," contingent on whether the county board of supervisors rezoned the remaining property to allow a few additional homes. Preservationists, developers, and tourism officials all supported the compromise, hailing it as a win-win-win scenario. The supervisors approved the change.

A total of 215 acres of the day-one battlefield now stand protected. Plantings to restore the wartime tree line will eventually provide a screen, blocking the development from view while providing additional privacy for the development's residents.

"Chancellorsville is flat-out one of our greatest victories," said one preservationist shortly after the compromise was struck. "We hold this up as a model of what happens when everyone works together for the greater good. It's a wonderful success story."

"CHANCELLORSVILLE IS FLAT-OUT ONE OF OUR GREATEST VICTORIES," SAID ONE PRESERVATIONIST SHORTLY AFTER THE COMPROMISE WAS STRUCK. "WE HOLD THIS UP AS A MODEL OF WHAT HAPPENS WHEN EVERYONE WORKS TOGETHER FOR THE GREATER GOOD."

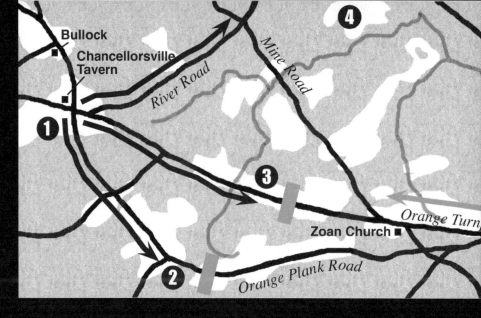

As elements of the Army of the Potomac branched out from the Chancellorsville intersection (1), Confederate forces under major generals Richard Anderson (2) and Lafayette McLaws (3) moved westward along parallel tracks to meet them. Stunned at first, Union forces regrouped and began to push the Confederates back. Along the northernmost route (4), Union Major General George Gordon Meade's Fifth Corps advanced unopposed into a position that would have allowed Meade to drop in behind the Confederates. Union commander Major General Joseph Hooker called his men back, though, into a defensive position back around the intersection. Today, a portion of the first day's battlefield, near (3) on the map, has been set aside by private preservation groups. Visitors can access the field from the westbound lane of Route 3. A walking trail covers part of the ground.

▶▶ TO STOP 4:

When you exit the parking lot, turn right onto Route 3 west. Travel 0.8 miles. Immediately as you crest the hill, you will see a left-hand turn for McLaws Drive. Pull into the median-crossing lane and stop. Cross Route 3 east. Please be watchful for oncoming traffic. Once on McLaws Drive, travel 0.4 miles to Stop 4.

The Second Battle of Chancellorsville ended in a compromise between developers, Spotsylvania County, and preservationists. As a result, portions of the ground where the first day's battle took place are now set preserved and interpreted for the public.

CHAPTER FOUR

SETTLING IN

The Furnace Road branched away from the Orange Turnpike toward the southwest. By the evening of May 1, Confederates set up their line parallel to the road.

Hooker convinced himself, and tried to convince his subordinates, that his rationale for pulling back was sound. "As the passage-way through the forest was narrow," he wrote, "I was satisfied that I could not throw troops fast enough to resist the advance of General Lee, and was apprehensive of being whipped in detail." His new position, on the other hand, would afford his men an excellent opportunity for victory. "I felt confident," he recalled later, "that I had eighty chances in a hundred to win."

That was hardly the kind of morale booster that engendered faith in his subordinates. Fifth Corps Commander George Gordon Meade, known by his men as a "google-eyed snapping turtle" for his looks as well as his disposition, would have none of it. "My God, if we can't hold the top of a hill, we certainly cannot hold the bottom of it!" he said. His protests fell on deaf ears.

The Federal army withdrew to a position anchored on the north near the intersection of Bullock Road and Ely's Ford Road. The line then looped in a wide arc out around Chancellorsville and back up, in a half-circle, to meet with the Orange Turnpike. From there, the Federal line extended westward along the Turnpike for two and a half miles. The entire position looked like a question mark, lying on its side.

Such a formation could not have been more appropriate. It perfectly matched the state of mind of nearly every Union corps commander.

Union Fifth Corps commander Major General George Gordon Meade.

★ ★ ★ ★ ★

As Federals settled into their new position around the Chancellorsville clearing, they repulsed several probing attacks from Confederates.

As the Union army pulled back, the Confederates moved forward to fill the vacuum left behind. By late afternoon, with the Union army hunkered down into their question mark-shaped line, the Confederates took up a position that stretched southwestward from the Turnpike down along Furnace Road—a byway that got its name because it led to one of the area's iron furnaces.

The Confederates weren't content to let their northern counterparts settle into their new position, though, and began to probe the Union line. "The rebs came over on the double-quick hollering like savages," one Union soldier said, "but we had 3 lines up ther[e] which stopped them very quick."

Jackson still wasn't ready to call it quits. He looked for a way around the Union position, sending troops all the way down the Furnace Road in the hopes that they could find access to a piece of high ground called Hazel Grove. The Union Twelfth Corps had beaten the Confederates to the hilltop, though. A sharp fight ensued. The Federals prevailed, but "we felt that we had our baptism of blood and commenced to realize the gravity of our position," one of them said.

Jackson had been watching the action from a nearby knoll with cavalry commander Jeb Stuart. Stuart ordered some of his artillery pieces to fire on Hazel Grove in an attempt to help dislodge the Federals, but Union artillery from Hazel Grove answered the artillery challenge and began to bombard the knoll. One of Stuart's staff members was killed, although Stuart and Jackson escaped unharmed.

And so ended the fighting on the first day. Nearly seven hundred men lay dead or wounded on the field. Joe Hooker's Army of the Potomac occupied the same basic position it had occupied the day before, but with one major difference: He now had the Army of Northern Virginia staring him squarely in the face.

McLaws Drive

TOUR STOP

McLAWS DRIVE RUNS PARALLEL TO THE EDGE OF A FIELD that saw more fighting during the battle of Chancellorsville than any other piece of ground on the battlefield—because it saw fighting on all three days of the battle.

On the first day, elements of the Union Second and Fifth Corps held the crest of the hill to cover the Federal pull-back. They eventually fell back, too. Puzzled by the Federal movement, Confederates tried twice to push forward, but stout Federal resistance indicated that the Union army had made a stand at the far side.

Major General Lafayette McLaws settled in along this stretch of the Confederate position. Ten artillery pieces set up along the ridge for support. On the second day of the battle, Lee ordered McLaws to demonstrate all along his line in an effort to hold the attention of the Federal Second Corps and, farther to the southwest, the Federal Twelfth Corps. "During that day and night and the next morning, I think we drove in their pickets ten or twelve times," wrote an officer from the

A hiking trail through the field north of McLaws Drive allows visitors to experience the rolling topography that proved deceptive for soldiers of both sides.

10th Georgia. The attacks kept Joe Hooker and his army distracted from Lee's true objective, and when events unfolded elsewhere on the battlefield late in the day, McLaws's demonstrations prevented Hooker from pulling troops from this part of his line to reinforce the collapse of the Union right flank.

On the morning of May 3, a Federal artilleryman felt encouraged by the previous day's action along this front. "The Rebels have got a good position," he admitted, "but we think we will make them skedaddle… Our men made two splendid charges last evening. We are all in good spirits. The boys all go into it with cheer. They go on for victory or death…[we have] great confidence in Fighting Jo. Hooker."

But it was the Confederate artillery that started the morning's fight. An artillery duel opened between Confederate gunners on Hazel Grove and Federal gunners at Fairview. Along the line here, McLaws also opened up with artillery. Lee ordered him and Anderson, located on McLaws's left flank, to push forward in an effort to connect with another wing of Lee's army. Pressed hard by the Confederates, the Federal line started to waver. Colonel Nelson Miles of the

61st New York Infantry rode out to steady his men when a bullet struck him in the stomach. "The result was an instant deathly sickening sensation," Miles wrote. "I was completely paralyzed below the waist. My horse seemed to realize what had occurred; he stopped, turned, and walked slowly back." Miles survived the wound and went on to eventually become general-in-chief of the Army during the Spanish-American War. His actions at Chancellorsville earned him the Congressional Medal of Honor.

Confederate Major General Lafayette McLaws.

McLaws' men drove their way across the field even as Hooker pulled back from his position around the Chancellorsville house. The Second Corps covered its own retreat skillfully, failing to let the Confederates swamp them.

On a map, the field looks like a clear spot in the midst of the heavily wooded Wilderness, but one Georgian called it the "thickest woods you ever saw." If you hike the one-mile interpretive trail across the field, you'll see that the topography is deceptive. The field has high ground to the east, but three distinct draws cut across the middle of the field, making it impossible to see what's really out there.

The draws also made convenient alleys for artillery fire. Confederate artillerymen placed across the turnpike to the north raked the flanks of advancing Union infantry hemmed in by the draws.

▶▶ TO STOP 5:

Continue down McLaws Drive for 0.4 miles and stop at the intersection with Old Plank Road, Route 610. Be watchful of oncoming traffic, and cross straight through the intersection. Continue driving straight, past the small clearing with the granite marker and the two cedar trees. Just beyond, on the right, you will see the parking area, located next to the trailhead. Follow the trail back to the site; for your safety, we recommend that you do not walk along the road.

CHAPTER FIVE

THE CRACKER BOX MEETING

Lee and Jackson sat around a campfire on a pair of cracker boxes and tried to determine a way to seize the initiative.

By the evening of May 1, Lee had made his headquarters near the intersection of the Plank and Furnace Roads. Jackson soon joined him to confer about possible courses of action. So quickly had they fallen into conversation that the two generals initially stood in the middle of the intersection to talk, but Union sharpshooters forced them off the road and into the protection of a small stand of cedars. There, seated on a fallen log, the two men continued their discussion.

Because of the success he'd had earlier in the day, Jackson was convinced Hooker had lost the will to fight. "By tomorrow morning," he said, "there will not be any of them left on this side of the river."

Lee wasn't so sure. Perhaps Hooker had consolidated his position in order to launch a concentrated strike. Perhaps he was drawing the Confederates into a trap. Perhaps he was refocusing his efforts for another attack in Fredericksburg. Perhaps….

Lee knew he needed more information. He sent one of Jackson's division commanders, Major General A.P. Hill, to find someone who might know the local terrain. Lee and Jackson also summoned their engineers. They sent out scouts. They discussed options. "How can we get at those people?" Lee mused aloud.

When Confederate cavalry commander Jeb Stuart rode into headquarters, he brought with him a piece of information that began to clarify the situation for Lee: The Union

JACKSON INTENDED TO
MARCH TWENTY-SEVEN
THOUSAND MEN OVER
TWELVE MILES OF DIRT
ROAD TO THE FAR FLANK
OF THE UNION ARMY.

right flank was stretched out along the Orange Turnpike with
nothing at its far end to protect it.

Lee already knew the Union army had secured its left
flank along the Rappahannock, so attacking there would be
impossible. An attack along the center would be difficult, especially since the Union army had spent the last few hours
fortifying that position. In that light, the Union right sounded
like a very tempting target—but how could Lee get his army
into position to attack there?

Stuart rode off to see what he could learn.

Lee and Jackson, meanwhile, leaned over Lee's wide map
and began to formulate their strategy.

* * * * *

As night crept toward morning, Lee and Jackson both felt
the tug of fatigue. The details of their plan would have to wait
until Stuart returned with his report. In the meantime, Lee
covered himself with his overcoat and stretched out for a nap
on a saddle blanket. Nearby, Jackson lay on the bare earth
beneath a tree; a staff member later covered him with a cape.

Jackson awoke two hours later feeling chilled from the
damp ground. He walked over to a nearby campfire that staff
members had built, sitting on an old army cracker box. His
chaplain, Reverend Beverly Tucker Lacy, whose family lived
in the area, sat down beside him.

Jackson explained the attack he wanted to make. Are there
any roads, he asked the chaplain, that the army could take to
get into position? Any of the routes he'd already considered
would likely bring the Confederate army too close to Federal
pickets, which would ruin any chance Jackson had at surprise.

Lacy knew someone who might be able to help: Charles
Wellford, who owned the nearby Catharine Furnace. Jackson
sent Lacy and mapmaker Jedadiah Hotchkiss to seek out
Wellford and gather what information he could. With
Wellford's help, Lacy and Hotchkiss "ascertained the roads
that led around to the enemy's rear," Hotchkiss wrote. In
fact, Wellford had recently cut a road through the Wilderness
that was so new it didn't show up on most of the maps.

When Hotchkiss returned to army headquarters, he found the generals sitting on a pair of cracker boxes that the Union army had abandoned there earlier in the day. Hotchkiss pulled up a cracker box to join them. He then traced out the twelve-mile route Wellford had shown him—a route that would take the army past the furnace, then south and west through hidden ways that then turned northwards and eventually linked with the Orange Turnpike just to the west of the Union right flank.

"General Jackson," asked Lee, "what do you propose to do?"

"Go around here," Jackson replied, indicating the route Hotchkiss had just traced.

"What do you propose to make this movement with?" Lee asked.

"My whole corps."

In other words, Jackson intended to march twenty-seven thousand men over twelve miles of dirt road to the far flank of the Union army.

"What will that leave me?" Lee asked.

"The divisions of Anderson and McLaws."

It was a huge gamble. Lee, with only thirteen thousand men, would have to keep Hooker's attention while Jackson marched into position.

Firelight flickered across Lee's face as he considered it. Silent moments passed.

"Well," the commander finally said, looking up at Jackson, "go on."

Jackson smiled.

Confederate cavalry commander Major General James Ewell Brown "Jeb" Stuart.

TOUR STOP **⑤**

Lee-Jackson Bivouac Site

IT HAS BECOME THE STUFF OF LEGENDS: THE TWO GREAT Confederate chieftains, Lee and Jackson, sitting on a pair of cracker boxes around a campfire, with orange-and-amber light flickering across their faces, mapping out an assault that would go down in the annals of history as one of the most crushing military blows ever delivered. Triumph and tragedy alike awaited them, though neither knew it, making the so-called "Cracker Box Meeting" especially portentous—and poignant.

Such a perspective, though, is only possible when seen through hindsight. Memory and irony have since imbued this meeting with a gravitas different than that which Lee and Jackson experienced. Certainly the two generals understood the seriousness of their situation, which of course gave their meeting an air of weightiness. But Lee and Jackson also understood that an important opportunity lay before them, and they were eager—even excited—to exploit it.

Today, a pair of cedar trees marks the site of the Cracker Box Meeting. The National Park Service planted the trees on October 23, 1937. Between them, set into a ground-level stone, a bronze plaque acknowledges the commemoration effort.

A two-foot-tall granite marker also adorns the site. Placed in 1903 by James Power Smith, an aide to General Jackson, the stone simply states: "Bivouac Lee & Jackson night of May 1, 1863." It's one of ten stones Smith placed to commemorate what he considered to be the most dramatic moments of the war that took place in Spotsylvania, Caroline, and Orange Counties.

The intersection where Lee and Jackson bivouacked as it looks today. The granite marker placed by James Power Smith stands in the foreground. The two cedars trees were planted on the site in 1937, with a bronze plaque set into the ground between them.

▶▶ TO STOP 6:

From Stop 5, proceed down the road 0.7 miles. On the right, you'll see a marker and a footpath leading to the birthplace of Matthew Fontaine Maury, the father of modern oceanography. Maury's story can be found in Appendix B.

To reach Stop 6, proceed past the Maury Birthplace site another 0.1 mile to the gap in the trees that stretches off to the right.

CHAPTER SIX

ON THE MARCH

When Lee and Jackson spoke privately on the morning of May 2, no one knew it would be their final meeting. Through hindsight, the encounter has become romanticized, as evidenced most notably in Everett Julio's highly symbolic painting.

Jackson's infantry had covered so much distance so quickly during the war that people had begun to call them "Jackson's Foot Cavalry."

On the morning of May 2, the foot cavalry stepped off shortly after seven-thirty, row after row of them—four by four by four by four—twenty-eight thousand strong.

The division of Brigadier General Robert Rodes led the march, followed by the division of Brigadier General Raleigh E. Colston. The third division, under Major General A.P. Hill, would bring up the rear.

As the head of the column passed the intersection of the Furnace and Plank Roads, Lee stood and watched them. Jackson, on horseback, rode up to speak briefly with his commander. They passed a few private words and then Jackson spurred his horse, Little Sorrel, onward. He rode along his column with his cap held high in the air in silent salute to his men, who waved their caps back at him in equal silence, trying to preserve the secrecy of their maneuver.

By eight o'clock, the column moved over a ridge near a little brick house. Beyond, the road began to descend to the low ground around Lewis's Run and Catharine Furnace. The contours of the land were such that the column, as it began its descent, was visible to Union artillerists who'd set up on the hilltop of Hazel Grove some three-quarters of a mile to the north. The artillerists' spotters, perched in treetops, noticed the butternut column snaking across the road and quickly

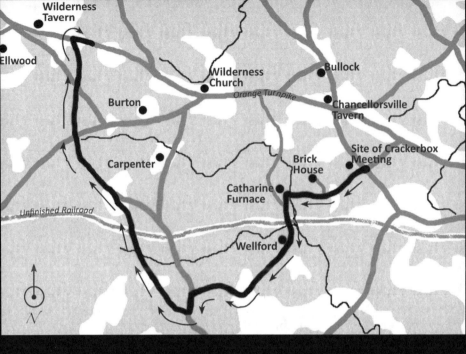

The route of Jackson's flank attack.

sent word to their commander that Rebels were afoot—but it would take almost two hours for the messages to move up the chain of command and for a response to return. Finally, word did come back, and at ten o'clock, a pair of Union cannon rolled into position and began blasting away at the Confederate column. Four other guns quickly joined in.

The cannonade harassed but did not harm the Confederate column. Jackson's men double-timed their way past the gap in the trees and continued down the road, down toward Lewis's Run and, ultimately, to Catharine Furnace beyond.

In the meantime, Jackson ordered his wagon train to take a wider route farther to the south to keep the wagons well beyond the range of the Union artillery.

His foot cavalry had been on the road for less than three hours, and already Jackson's secret march wasn't so secret.

Jackson's Foot Cavalry marched past the bivouac site toward Catharine Furnace along the Furnace Road.

The Gap in the Trees

THE GAP IN THE TREES A VISITOR SEES TODAY LOOKS MUCH different than it did in 1863. The National Park Service maintains the gap to show visitors the contours of the land in the direction of Hazel Grove. However, the trees today stand much taller than they did at the time of the battle. The Wilderness consisted of short, scrubby bushes, and the immature trees that hardly loomed as high as today's oaks and pines. The shorter tree cover offered a much clearer line of site in the direction of Hazel Grove.

Still, Confederates only had to march through the exposed position for a few yards before the tree cover and topography blocked them from sight again. The gap in the trees today represents the approximate distance and position that the Confederates had to cross under fire. Although the Union artillerists were essentially shooting down a narrow alley, their distant position made it difficult to fire with much accuracy even though their 10-pounder Parrotts had rifled barrels. (Rifling, whether in cannons or in muskets, typically allowed for greater accuracy because it put a spin on the projectile, which kept it moving on a straighter path.)

Today, the gap in the trees does not offer the same unobstructed view to Hazel Grove that it did in 1863, but visitors can still get a sense of how exposed Confederates were as they crossed through.

Union gunners at Hazel Grove took aim at Jackson's column shortly after the secret march began.

▶▶ **TO STOP 7:**

From Stop 6, proceed down the road 0.6 miles to the remains of Catharine Furnace. Park in the small lot on the left-hand side of the road, opposite the remains of the old furnace stack.

CHAPTER SEVEN

CATHARINE FURNACE

Once a bustling industrial complex, all that remains of Catharine Furnace today are the ruins of the furnace itself.

Charles C. Wellford had made a good life for himself as a merchant in Fredericksburg, but when the armies converged on the city in December 1862, Wellford moved his family west to a property he owned in Spotsylvania County in the middle of The Wilderness.

Wellford's property sat near another of his business interests, Catharine Furnace. Originally built in 1837, Catharine Furnace operated for a decade before shutting down, only to fire up again at the start of the war to help process iron ore for the Confederacy.

To import ore for the furnace, Wellford had recently cut a new road through the Wilderness. It was this new road, which ran south from the furnace, that Wellford had told Stuart and Lacy about the previous night. To the north, a road ran from the furnace toward Hazel Grove.

The Confederate column reached the intersection shortly after eight o'clock. The area all around the furnace, which had been cleared of timber, "gave an open reach and fully exposed the moving column to view," a Union officer later said. Indeed, Union gunners had spotted the Confederate movement, but by this point, they had not yet opened fire on the column.

Jackson worried that the Federals might send scouts—or something worse—from Hazel Grove toward the furnace. Jackson detailed the lead regiment from his column, the 23rd Georgia commanded by Colonel Emory Best, to fall out of line and take up a defensive position some 300 yards north of

Charles Wellford, owner of Catharine Furnace.

The Catharine Furnace complex featured a variety of buildings and employed a variety of skilled and unskilled workers, including as many as seventy slaves.

Union Third Corps commander Major General Daniel Sickles.

the intersection. The Georgians would serve as a screen, holding back any Union attempts to probe ahead.

The rest of the column, meanwhile, hurried south past the furnace on the newly cut road.

★ ★ ★ ★ ★

By one o'clock, Dan Sickles could hardly contain himself. The major general commanding the Union Third Corps had heard reports of Confederates marching south of his position for almost five hours. At mid-morning he'd given the okay for his artillery to fire on them, but now he wanted more. For the past two hours, he'd been pressing Joe Hooker for permission to advance against the Confederates.

Hooker finally unleashed him. "Advance cautiously toward the road followed by the enemy, and harass the movement as much as possible," Hooker ordered.

But Sickles planned for a bolder move. He first sent in a regiment of sharpshooters followed by a full brigade.

Sickles had no way to know it, but nearly all of the Confederate column had by now made its way safely past the furnace on the road south and west. Only a few artillery pieces had yet to pass. The Georgians, still in place to the north of the intersection as a precaution, held their ground

An iron pig produced at
Catharine Furnace.

against the advancing sharpshooters long enough for the final
elements of the column to clear the area.

As the Federals continued to push forward, the Georgians
fell back to the furnace itself, taking up position around one of
the property's outbuildings. Confederate artillery support
slowed the Federal advance even further. But still the Federals
pushed—and they had numbers on their side. The Georgians,
realizing their position was ultimately untenable, continued to
fall back down the road.

The firefight—tough and determined on both sides—
soon attracted additional attention.

Catharine Furnace

TOUR STOP ⑦

THE MAIN STACK OF THE FURNACE STILL STANDS AS THE
last remaining sentry of what was once a bustling enterprise.
When the furnace was in operation, between six and ten
buildings dotted the open landscape here.

The furnace stack stood thirty-six feet tall. It measured
thirty feet square at the base and nineteen feet square at the
top, with thick fieldstone walls. Behind the stack, a dock
stretched from the crest of the hill to the stack's open maw.
Workers would wheel cartloads of raw ore across the dock
and dump it down into the tower. With a full fire going, the
temperature inside reached 2,800 degrees. The ore would
melt down, and workers would add lime to help separate the
impurities from the molten iron. The resulting slag was
skimmed off and hauled away; much of it was dumped into
the woods across the road. Meanwhile, workers poured the
remaining iron into molds to create bars, also called "pigs,"
that could then be transported off-site for processing.

Today, the stack is all that
remains of Catharine Furnace.

After crossing through the gap in the trees, Furnace Road took Jackson's men downhill and across Lewis's Run.

Anywhere between sixty and seventy slaves might be employed to excavate the ore, cut the wood, haul the materials, and operate the furnace itself. The enterprise also employed a manager and various skilled and unskilled workers.

They would typically fire up the furnace for a four, or five, month period, called a blast, when the furnace would be in production; during the remaining part of the year, workers usually farmed.

Catharine Furnace was one of several such furnaces—the first dating back as early as 1718—established in this region because of the rich supplies of iron ore and the abundant supply of timber. The forests in the area had once been virtually clear-cut to provide fuel for those furnaces, some of which could consume 750 acres worth of timber in a single year. By those standards, Catharine Furnace was modest; it consumed perhaps one hundred acres' worth of timber per year. It produced approximately two tons of processed iron for every acre of timber it burned. The furnace property included 4,648 adjacent acres.

Although fighting swirled around the furnace complex on May 2, a story—probably apocryphal—from a local family tells of the wife of a Confederate soldier who sought shelter at the furnace because she was going into labor just as the battle was getting under way. A Confederate lieutenant, John Morgan, discovered the woman and her sensitive condition, and realized that she was physically unable to evacuate with the area's other civilians. Morgan "assigned six of his patrol to circle the house continuously with white flags until the battle was over." Although the actual identity of the lieutenant has never been confirmed, two likely candidates exist: John G. Morgan of the 45th Georgia Infantry or J.D. Morgan, a surgeon with the 23rd Georgia, both of whom came from regiments posted at or near the furnace. In any event, as the story goes, the woman honored the officer by naming her baby Morgan Lieutenant Monroe.

The remains of the furnace stack.

After the battle of Chancellorsville, the armies passed out of the area for a time, but in May of 1864, General George Armstrong Custer and his cavalry paid a visit to the furnace. The cavalry destroyed it, but the Wellfords quickly had their operation up and running again, and they continued to process iron for the Confederate war effort until the end of the war. With its biggest customer gone, Catharine Furnace ceased operations shortly thereafter, marking the end of an era.

▶▶ **TO STOP 8:**

From Stop 7, proceed down the road 0.6 miles. Park in the small pull-off on the right-hand side of the road.

CHAPTER EIGHT

WITHDRAWALS

————◆————

Even as Jackson's Foot Cavalry marched past the Wellford homestead, Union forces began to harass the rear of the Confederate column back by Catharine Furnace.

As Jackson's long line of butternut soldiers moved past the Wellford house, the Wellfords, too, were moving, loading their belongings into carts and wagons in preparation for a quick escape.

Near the head of the column marched young Charles Wellford, who, at the behest of his father, had agreed to serve as a guide for the army. Jeb Stuart had made his headquarters in the family's yard the day before and knew the family could provide crucial intelligence.

Stuart's men had not been the first to visit the family, though. On April 30, Federal soldiers on a foraging mission had swept across the Wellfords' property. "The Yankees were down at the Furnace not a mile from us, indeed all around they were shouting and shooting," wrote Evelina Wellford, the elder Charles' niece, in a letter to her sister, "and we four unprotected females every moment expecting their appearance at the house. As soon as they came so near, uncle [Charles] and Charlie made their escape into the woods, as they certainly would have been captured had they remained."

About twenty Federals finally dropped in, "searching the house for arms and Confederates, shooting the fowls, and stealing provisions, of which we had a scant supply," Evelina said, conceding that they generally behaved very well. "They seemed confident of success…of course we were amused at their boasting," she wrote.

As the Federals left and Stuart first arrived, a late-night skirmish resulted in a single casualty, a major from Richmond, who was brought back to the Wellford house, where he died overnight.

Now, two days later, with twenty-eight thousand soldiers marching past the house, more turmoil was brewing. "In expectation of some trouble the carts were waiting at the door," Evelina recalled, "and our trunks and some other valuables being put in, and sent off, we hurriedly took our departure for the woods, making as good time as you might imagine under the circumstances."

As the Wellfords made their departure, Federal artillery set up near the furnace. "The shells came whizzing by, bursting apparently near us," Evelina wrote, "and you may judge that our feelings were not of the most comfortable kind."

Off they fled into "a strange woody country, perfectly ignorant of where the path we were taking would lead us to...."

★ ★ ★ ★ ★

Even as the Wellfords were leaving, the Federal army was advancing down the road—with members of the 23rd Georgia, flushed out of their cover at the Catharine Furnace, trying to stave them off. Under heavy pressure, the Georgians fell back all the way to an unfinished railroad cut that lined the north edge of the Wellford farm. There, they fended off the Federal troops, but the weight of numbers was against them. Union sharpshooters worked their way around to the right flank of the Georgians' positions and hit them as they were pinned in the cut.

The Georgians' colonel, Emory Best, ordered his men to fall back again, but few of his men received the order. Rather than wait to ensure they obeyed, Best made off to the rear, leaving most of his men behind. Some 269 members of the regiment would end up as prisoners. Best would later be court-martialed for abandoning his men and was drummed out of the army.

The Georgians, however, remained defiant even as prisoners. "You may think you have done a big thing just now, but wait till Jackson gets round on your right," one of them boasted. "You'll catch hell before night," said another.

Union Third Corps commander Dan Sickles seemed unconcerned by any of it. While the Wellford family had seen trouble marching down the road, Dan Sickles saw it as something entirely different.

"I think it is a retreat," he said.

Although he'd been ordered not to bring on a general engagement, Sickles was itching for a fight. He ordered more men to move southward from Hazel Grove toward the furnace. He also moved a division into position for support.

As the afternoon wore on, Sickles called for still more reinforcements. Closest at hand was Major General Oliver Otis Howard, standing in reserve with his Eleventh Corps. Sickles sent a message to Howard that "he was about to make a grand attack, having been for some time driving the enemy, and expected soon a brilliant result; that he desired to place [Howard's] reinforcement upon his right flank in the forward movement." Howard personally led a division down toward the action, deciding he should be on hand in case things were really as bad as Sickles was making them out to be.

"The expedition to the Wellford Furnace and below is clearly the cause of the failure of the campaign," wrote Dr. Augustus Hamlin, an Eleventh Corps surgeon who later became one of the earliest historians of the battle. "[Hooker] permitted twenty thousand men to be detached from the entrenched lines of defense and moved forward two or three miles in a dense forest, leaving a gap of three miles" between the rest of Howard's Eleventh Corps and the right flank of Sickles' position.

That three-mile gap, though no one suspected it at the time, would prove disastrous for the Union army.

Colonel Emory Best of the 23rd Georgia Infantry.

TOUR STOP ⑧

The Wellford Home and the Unfinished Railroad Cut

Today, the unfinished railroad cut is largely overgrown, although the banks of the cut are clearly visible in many spots. Visitors standing on Jackson Trail East can best find it by looking for a gated right-of-way just inside the treeline from the Wellford home site. The railroad cut runs parallel along the north (right) edge of the right-of-way.

FROM THE PARKING AREA, IF YOU WALK BACK DOWN THE road one-tenth of a mile, you'll come to the unfinished railroad cut where the Georgians made their last stand.

The railroad was cut in the early 1850s as a path linking Fredericksburg to Orange Court House, but competition from the Orange Plank Road, which runs a nearly parallel route just a few miles to the west, proved to be the railroad's undoing, and the project never saw completion prior to the war.

During the 1864 Battle of the Wilderness, James Longstreet would send Confederate soldiers down the railroad cut just a few miles southwest of here to spearhead a flank attack on the Union army near the Brock Road/Plank Road intersection. One of the brigade commanders involved in that attack, William Mahone, had been one of the railroad's initial developers.

In the post-war years, the railroad was completed, operating for more than sixty years before going bankrupt for a second time. The tracks were torn up in the late 1930s. Today the cut is still visible, and closer to the city of Fredericksburg, Spotsylvania County even converted part of the line into a bike and walking path.

If you walk back to the parking area, a footpath will lead you to the former site of the Wellford home. Besides owning Catharine Furnace, the Wellfords owned 600 acres of improved land and 629 acres of unimproved land. Charles also owned eleven slaves. James Diggs, an overseer, also lived on the property.

"We lost a great deal by their occupation, but not as much as we expected," Evelina Wellford wrote in her letter to her sister. "[U]ncle C he has lost nearly all his clothes, aunt Mary too, but his books are saved and the Furnace too, so we have still have much to be thankful for." A few more such moves by the army, she feared, "will just break us up entirely."

Families that did not flee as the Wellfords did found themselves with unwanted company. The Chancellors, for instance, had the commanding general of the Union army commandeer their home for his headquarters. Thomas Downer, a farmer who lived with his family in the Hawkins House near the Wilderness Church, found himself "hosting" Union General Carl Schurz and his staff. While everyone treated each other "very kindly and hospitably," Downer's family were essentially captives.

ONE OF THE BRIGADE COMMANDERS INVOLVED IN THAT ATTACK, WILLIAM MAHONE, HAD BEEN ONE OF THE RAILROAD'S INITIAL DEVELOPERS.

▶▶ **TO STOP 9:**

From Stop 8, proceed along Jackson Trail East for another 2 miles.

As you continue on from this point along Jackson Trail East, you'll see instances where modern development is encroaching on the edges of the battlefield. While the National Park Service owns the road itself and maintains it as a public road, in some places the Park Service's property stretches only ten feet on either side of the road. That's why you'll see some homes built so close to the flank march route. (In other places, the Park Service owns more of the land.)

Follow Jackson Trail East until you come to the intersection with Brock Road. Use caution as you turn left, following Brock Road for 0.3 miles. Pay particular attention to the dips in the road since they play an important role in understanding the next phase of Jackson's flank movement. You will see Jackson Trail West on the right-hand side. Turn onto Jackson Trail West and pull over into the parking area on the right-hand side of the road.

The Wellford family lived in a home that once sat in a clearing next to the road now known as Jackson Trail East.

CHAPTER NINE

JACKSON'S FLANK MARCH

PART ONE

A Union soldier once described the Wilderness as "a region of gloom and the shadow of death." Another said, "The scrawny, moss-tagged pines, the garroted alders, the hoary willows give a very sad look to these wet thickets."

As the Confederate column reached the intersection with the Brock Road, young Charles Wellford led Jackson and his men left, toward the south, away from the Union army. The terrain of the southward route offered concealment from Federal observers. Confederates marched over a quick series of rolls and dips in the Brock Road before coming to a private road that plunged into the thick woods on the right. The column turned onto this new road, its movement hidden from view by the small hills the soldiers had just crossed.

But just as the terrain protected the Confederates from view, it also prevented them from seeing much. "For hours at the time we neither saw nor heard anything," one marcher wrote.

The soldiers didn't know the specifics of their mission, but they sensed that something big was unfolding. "Every man in the ranks knew that we were engaged in some great flank movement," said Dr. Hunter Holmes McGuire, Jackson's surgeon, "and they eagerly responded and pressed on at a rapid gait."

Jackson urged his men to keep up their pace and keep the ranks closed. Regimental commanders were ordered to march at the rear of their regiments to minimize straggling. "Strict silence was enforced, the men being allowed to speak only in whispers," one North Carolinian said.

Cartographer Jedediah
Hotchkiss sketched out this
map of Chancellorsville for
Jackson's use.

The men marched about one mile every twenty-five minutes, with a ten-minute break each hour to rest.

One artillerist noted how "grave & silent" Jackson looked. McGuire, too, noticed it. "Never will I forget the eagerness and intensity of Jackson on that march to Hooker's rear," McGuire recalled. "His face was pale, his eyes flashing. Out from his thin, compressed lips came the terse command: 'Press forward, press forward.' In his eagerness, as he rode, he leaned over the neck of his horse as if in that way the march might be hurried."

On and on he urged them. "Press forward," Jackson said. "Press forward."

Jackson Trail West

TOUR STOP 9A

THE WELL-GRADED GRAVEL ROAD YOU SEE TODAY IS A FAR cry from the narrow, primitive path the Confederate column had to follow for much of its way in the spring of 1863. Two cars can pass each other along the road today, but four infantrymen, walking shoulder to shoulder, had just enough space to move.

Keep in mind that the forest you see is much more open than it was back then, too. Union Major General Oliver Otis Howard, who would be getting a visit from Jackson's men in the very near future, described the Wilderness of Spotsylvania County as an area filled with "stunted trees, such as scraggy oaks, bushy firs, cedars, and junipers, all entangled with a thick, almost impenetrable undergrowth, and criss-crossed with an abundance of wild vines." That dense underbrush felt like an oppressive wall crowding in on the sides of the road as vegetation reached into the open space for whatever sunlight it could get.

A postwar view of the Orange Turnpike near the position where the Union Eleventh Corps was posted.

The route of Jackson's troops through the dense thickets of the Wilderness helped keep the movement hidden from Union eyes.

Today, Jackson Trail is much wider than it was in 1863, when there was hardly room for four men to march side by side.

Continue along Jackson Trail West for 1 mile until you reach Poplar Run. Park along the gravel pull-off just before the road crosses the stream. If you get out of your vehicle, be cautious of any oncoming vehicles that might be coming from either direction; it is not a heavily traveled road, but there is some traffic on it.

PART TWO

"The day was very warm, the route poor," wrote Lieutenant Octavius Wiggins of the 37th North Carolina. Wiggins, as a member of Jackson's Foot Cavalry, had participated in a number of Old Jack's famous foot races. "[T]his differed from all others I had ever known in severity.... On we rushed, jumping bushes, branches, up and down hill."

Temperatures climbed into the eighties. McGuire and other medical officers soon found themselves attending to soldiers falling out of line from heat stroke.

If the heat bothered Jackson, he never showed it. In fact, he wore a heavy India-rubber raincoat over his uniform jacket all day. Although he made no mention of it to anyone, he had caught a chill over the previous few days. Dr. McGuire, off

assisting swooning marchers, was too busy to notice.

The only thing that might have made the march even more unpleasant would have been dust. Dust on the march choked a man and got in his eyes. Fortunately for Jackson's marchers, recent rain kept the dust down—although it also left mudholes in some of the low spots.

It was therefore a welcome sight when the column came down the hill toward Poplar Run. While the column didn't stop, soldiers were allowed to quench their thirst in the stream as they trod through.

They followed the road up and away from the stream, pressing forward, pressing forward.

Recent rains kept the dust down along the march route, which made the trek more bearable. Still, temperatures soared into the high eighties as the day wore on, making it an uncomfortable march for most soldiers.

As troops descended the hill toward Poplar Run, they welcomed the sight of water— the first they'd passed on that hot day since Lewis's Run near Catharine Furnace.

TOUR STOP Poplar Run

Poplar Run marked approximately the halfway point for the marching column.

"Never will I forget the eagerness and intensity of Jackson on that march to Hooker's rear," recalled Jackson's surgeon. "His face was pale, his eyes flashing. Out from his thin, compressed lips came the terse command: 'Press forward, press forward.'"

POPLAR RUN TODAY IS LITTLE MORE THAN A TRICKLE running across some cobblestones. From here, it flows east. Near the Wellford house site, it links with Lewis' Run and flows south to eventually become the Ni River, which in turn flows southeast and joins with several other tributaries to become the Mattaponi River.

When rain swept through the region in late April of 1863, rivers and streams rose quickly. They were high enough, for instance, to delay a cavalry raid by Union Major General George Stoneman, who couldn't cross the rain-swollen waterways. But by May 2, water levels had dropped. Poplar Run was easily fordable.

Today, heavy rainfalls occasionally push Poplar Run's water levels as high as three or four feet, but such occasions are rare. Typically, at its deepest points, the water is usually only shin deep.

From here, as you travel farther along Jackson Trail West, you'll pass a large farm on the left. In 1863, that area was still thick wilderness. Just down the road on the right, you'll pass a subdivision built in the 1990s. For being a path chosen for its remoteness, the Jackson Trail today continues to become less and less remote in the face of development pressure.

About nine-tenths of a mile from Poplar Run, you'll see on the left the remains of trench lines, which run parallel to the road. Federal soldiers dug these trenches during the Battle of the Wilderness in May 1864.

Continue along Jackson Trail West another 1.2 miles. You will reach another intersection with Brock Road. Park in the pull-off area on the left side of Jackson Trail West; do NOT yet travel onto Brock Road. If you get out of your vehicle, be cautious of any oncoming traffic.

Near this spot, where Jackson Trail West today intersects with Brock Road, Jackson met up with Confederate cavalryman Fitzhugh Lee, who had been scouting in advance of the column.

Jackson originally planned to turn right at the intersection with the Orange Plank Road, but information from Fitz Lee persuaded him to continue along Brock Road in order to get all the way around the Union flank.

PART THREE

By 1:30 in the afternoon, as the tail end of his column finally filed past Catharine Furnace, the head of the column reached Brock Road. By two o'clock, it neared the intersection with the Orange Plank Road. There, Jackson planned to form his twenty-eight thousand men into line of battle and sweep up the Orange Plank Road and into the Union flank.

But Brigadier General Fitzhugh Lee of the cavalry—and Robert E. Lee's nephew—arrived with news. He invited Jackson to follow him along a narrow pathway through the woods, where they came to a cleared hilltop near a farmhouse.

"What a sight presented itself before me!" Fitz Lee later wrote. "Below, and but a few hundred yards distant, ran the Federal line of battle.... There were the lines of defense, with abatis in front, and long lines of stacked arms in the rear. Two cannon were visible in the part of the line...The soldiers were in groups in the rear, laughing, chatting, smoking, probably engaged, here and there, in games of cards, and other amusements indulged in while feeling safe and comfortable, awaiting orders. In rear of them were other parties driving up and butchering beeves."

The problem, as Fitz Lee pointed out, was that the Orange Plank Road, which Jackson had originally intended as his avenue of attack, ran straight into the line of Union entrenchments, not into the Union flank. But from his hilltop vantage point, the two men could see the end of the Union line less than a mile or so farther to the west. If Jackson followed the new route suggested by the cavalryman, he could still swing his army into the Union flank with plenty of cover from the Wilderness to shield his moves.

"Stonewall's face bore an expression of intense interest during the five minutes he was on the hill," Fitz Lee said. "The paint of approaching battle was coloring his cheeks, and he was radiant to find no preparation had been made to guard against a flank attack."

Jackson rode back to his column and began barking out orders. His lead division must move ahead toward the turn-pike; Jackson promised to join them shortly. The Stonewall

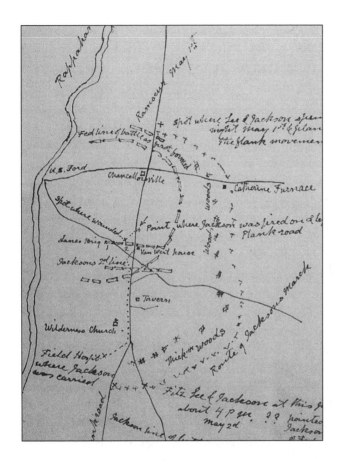

Following the war, Jackson's brother-in-law, Joseph Morrison, who had served on the general's staff and was on the Mountain Road at the time of Jackson's wounding, made a sketch of the battlefield and the route of the flank movement.

Brigade, under Brigadier General Frank Paxton, must stay with Fitz Lee's cavalry along the Orange Plank Road to guard the Confederate flank as it passed by.

It was just before 3:00 p.m., and Jackson penned a quick dispatch to his commander. In four sentences, he reported that his lead division was up and the next two appeared to be well on their way. He also confirmed the position of the Union army.

"I hope as soon as practicable to attack," Jackson wrote. "I trust that an Ever Kind Providence will bless us with great success."

TOUR STOP # Reconnaissance Point

EVEN JED HOTCHKISS, JACKSON'S MAPMAKER, WHO HAD AN excellent reputation for his work, understood that the Confederate army was moving through a poorly mapped area. It wasn't called the Wilderness for nothing. That's why Jackson relied so heavily on local guides like young Charles Wellford. He also knew that he might have to adjust his plan on the fly as the situation became clearer. It's no surprise, then, that his trip to the hill at the Burton Farm—about a mile and a quarter almost due north (and just slightly east) from your current position—led to a quick change in plan.

The Union Army had observation points of its own. One such observation point was the Carpenter homestead, which sat a little less than a mile and a half due northeast of your current position along a road called Brook Road. Brook Road—called Herndon Road today, it doesn't show up on the Park Service maps—provided an open shot from the Union line almost straight down to Brock Road. Had the Confederate column marched north on Brock Road, back where Jackson Trail East first intersects it, the column would've marched in plain sight within a thousand yards of the Carpenter homestead. The more circuitous route kept the Confederates hidden.

On the way to Stop 10, you'll come to an intersection with Orange Plank Road. Jackson had originally planned to turn right at the intersection, but after his reconnaissance trip with Fitz Lee, he chose to go straight.

A left turn at the intersection would bring you to the spot where Confederate Lieutenant General James Longstreet was accidentally wounded by his own men on May 6, 1864, during the Battle of the Wilderness—one year and four days after Jackson was wounded under similar circumstances less than four miles away. The intersection itself was a key objective of both armies during the fighting that day.

▶▶ TO STOP 10:

Go north on the Brock Road. Traffic on the Brock Road can be difficult to see as it approaches, so please use caution. Follow Brock Road 1.1 miles to the intersection with the Orange Plank Road. Go straight through the intersection and follow the road another 1.4 miles until you come to the intersection with Route 3. Turn right onto Route 3 east and travel 1.6 miles. You will see a turning lane on the left. Pull into the turning lane and then prepare to turn left onto Route 3 west. When traffic is clear, pull onto Route 3 west and travel 0.1 miles. You will see a sign on the right for Jackson's Flank Attack. Pull onto the gravel lane and drive 0.1 mile to the parking area at the end.

CHAPTER TEN
THE ATTACK

Eleventh Corps commander Major General Oliver Otis Howard.

Confederate Major General Ambrose Powell "A. P." Hill.

The march was nearly over, but the race was still on. It was just after five o'clock, and daylight would linger for only a few hours more. Jackson needed to get his attack underway while there was still time to exploit his advantage.

Of his twenty-eight thousand men, two-thirds of them had arrived on the field and gotten into position. The division of Brigadier General Robert Rodes would lead the attack. His battle line, two men deep, shoulder to shoulder, stretched nearly a mile beyond the Orange Turnpike in each direction, nearly ten thousand men in all. Lined up two hundred yards behind Rodes, Brigadier General Raleigh Colston's division would follow as support, nearly eight thousand strong.

But the majority of Jackson's third division, under Major General A.P. Hill, was still on the march. If Jackson waited for them, he'd lose precious daylight. Those men, he decided, would be used to support the advance as they became available.

Jackson sent word to his subordinates that they would launch the attack at 5:15 p.m. Once under way, he told them, "under no circumstances was there to be any pause in the advance"—easier said than done in the Wilderness, with its rolling terrain and dense tangle of underbrush.

While that dense tangle continued to provide cover for the Confederates, even more invaluable to them as protection was Joe Hooker's continued belief that the Confederate army was in retreat. "We know that the enemy is fleeing, trying to save his trains," Hooker said in a telegraph as late as 4:10 that

83

"We emerged charging with a yell over their cooking detail," wrote one Confederate, **"routing their rear line which retreated with firing only a few shots at us...."**

afternoon. When a Union picket sent word up the chain of command that "a large body of the enemy is massing in my front"—along with the plea, "For God's sake make dispositions to receive them"—the report was ignored.

If Hooker was erroneous in his assumptions, Eleventh Corps Commander Oliver Otis Howard was downright confused. All day, he had received conflicting reports from Union headquarters about what was expected of him. During a personal inspection of the Eleventh Corps' line, Hooker had lauded Howard's troops and their dispositions, although he also asked Howard to move some men around. Howard complied, turning several units to face west as protection for the flank. Later, Hooker sent word to Howard that the Confederates were retreating, and Hooker ordered Howard to send reinforcements to help Sickles nab the retreating Confederates at Catharine Furnace. Howard, like all other corps commanders, had even received orders to "replenish your supplies of forage, provisions, and ammunition to be ready to start at an early hour tomorrow." Hooker planned to chase after retreating Confederates tomorrow, not fight them today.

"I was deceived at the time of Jackson's attack," Howard later admitted, "and did believe, with all the other officers, that he was making for Orange Court House."

Headquarters flag for the Union Eleventh Corps.

Not everyone in the Eleventh Corps was so sure. Some troops began to get edgy. Most of their commanders urged them not to get so worked up—it was probably just a few bushwackers moving around out in the forest, they said. Other commanders, though, quietly began to shift their men around to face not south but west. "Some of us will not see another sunrise," predicted one Ohio colonel.

Among soldiers in both armies, the tension and anticipation grew as thick as the Wilderness itself, yet Jackson himself betrayed no such feelings. "There sat Gen. Jackson on Little Sorrel as calm as if sitting upon the seashore a thousand miles from the battlefield," observed one officer.

At 5:15, Jackson turned to his lead division commander. "Are your men ready, General Rodes?"

"Yes, sir!"

"You may go forward then."

★ ★ ★ ★ ★

"In my youth," wrote Howard years after the battle,

my brother and I had a favorite spot in an upper field of my father's farm from which we were accustomed, after the first symptoms of a coming storm, to watch the operations of the contending winds;

Union batteries commanded by Captain Hubert Dilger tried to stem the Confederate attack.

Union Artillery Captain Hubert Dilger had faced his batteries west—among the only Union soldiers in position to defend against Jackson's attack.

the sudden gusts and whirlwinds; the sideling swallows excitedly seeking shelter; the swift and swifter, black and blacker clouds, ever rising higher and pushing their angry fronts toward us. As we listened we heard the low rumbling from afar; as the storm came nearer the woods bent forward and shook fiercely their thick branches; the lightning zigzagged in flashes, and the deep-bassed thunder echoed more loudly, till there was scarcely an interval between its ominous crashing discharges.

In some such manner came on that battle of May 2d.

Its first lively effects, like a cloud of dust driven before a coming shower, appeared in the startled rabbits, squirrels, quail, and other game flying wildly hither and thither in evident terror, and escaping, where possible, into adjacent clearings....

Most Union soldiers had been settling down to cook dinner, with their arms stacked. The unexpected bounty of game that came bounding out of the woods seemed a pleasant surprise—until the Rebel Yell erupted.

And so it was that Howard's Eleventh Corps was largely unprepared for the Confederate juggernaut that swept out of the woods and into the Union army's exposed right flank.

"Jackson was on us," said one Union soldier, "and fear was on us."

"It was a terrible gale!" Howard wrote.

The rush, the rattle, the quick lightning from a hundred points at once; the roar, redoubled by echoes through the forest....

[M]ore quickly than it could be told, with all the fury of the wildest hailstorm, everything, every sort of organization that lay in the path of the mad current of panic-stricken men, had to give way and be broken into fragments.

Howard, who had only one arm, tucked a Union flag under his amputated stump in a desperate attempt to rally his startled men as they stampeded away from Jackson's attacking forced.

The few Union cannon that had been pointed westward offered little help in stemming the Confederate tide, mostly because their infantry support abandoned them. Farther back, reserve cannon were blocked out of the fight because the fleeing mass of soldiers blocked their line of fire.

On horseback, Howard grabbed a U.S. flag and tried to rally his troops. Several units answered his call. The first line of Federal defense, near the Wilderness Church, quickly collapsed, but Colonel Adolphus Bushbeck's 154th New York set up a second line of defense a few hundred yards to the east. The five thousand or so men in this line held on for perhaps twenty minutes before the full brunt of Jackson's attack overwhelmed them.

In their flight, the Union Eleventh Corps, comprised largely of German-Americans, became know as "the Flying Dutchmen."

Because Sickles had relocated the bulk of his Third Corps to the south for his sparring match near Catharine Furnace, Howard's men were separated from the rest of the Federal army with no one to back them up. The Confederates, therefore, had plenty of room to simply keep pushing the Federals.

Despite the cacophony of the Eleventh Corps's collapse, no one at Federal headquarters two miles to the east heard a thing. Their first indication of the disaster came when a flood of fugitives suddenly streamed past the Chancellor mansion. Some of the fleeing soldiers continued down the Turnpike through the lines of the Union Twelfth Corps on the far side, where they were captured by Confederates in McLaws's division.

Union artillerist Thomas Osborn hoped that such a sight "may never again be seen in the Federal Army of the United States…Aghast and terror-stricken, heads bare and panting for breath, they pleaded like infants at the mother's breast that we should let them pass unhindered."

Hooker snapped into action. To stem the tide and prevent the panic from spreading, he ordered men of the Twelfth Corps to shoot anyone else who tried to flee. He also ordered a military band, positioned nearby, to begin playing inspirational music. Hooker then repositioned the reserve artillery around

the Chancellor house so that it aimed westward to meet the oncoming Confederate horde, and he manned one of the guns himself to lead by example. He told the infantry stationed nearby to get ready to throw themselves into the breach.

"Receive the enemy on your bayonets!" he ordered.

The Wilderness Church, shortly after the time of the battle.

★ ★ ★ ★ ★

Jackson, meanwhile, continued to urge his men on: "Press forward. Press forward."

But the Wilderness itself made that harder and harder to do. Some Confederate units, meeting less resistance from Federal defenders and having an easier time moving through the brush, advanced farther than others. Some units, advancing straight forward while others had to follow the rolls and swales of the land, advanced more rapidly than others. Units got confused, entangled, disoriented.

Twilight settled in. The thick shadows in the woods deepened. The full moon just peeked over the treetops. One general said it cast "just enough of its light to make darkness visible."

Jackson's advance stalled. He called back for A.P. Hill, whose troops had brought up the rear of the march and were now available as reserves. Jackson planned to resume the attack as soon as his men were reorganized and Hill's reserves ready. To get a clearer sense of the tactical situation, he and his staff rode ahead of the main line to do some reconnaissance.

His trip, which would take him down the Mountain Road, would prove more fateful than he would have ever imagined.

Chronologically, the story of Jackson's wounding told in the prologue takes place at this point.

TOUR STOP # Jackson's Flank Attack

IT MIGHT BE HARD TO IMAGINE HOW LONG JACKSON'S BATTLE line was when the Confederates got into position. If you stand near the cluster of signs and look to the north, you'll see a line of trees a couple hundred yards away. If you look to the south, past Route 3, you can see more trees. The restricted view makes it tough to get a sense of how long the Confederate battle line stretched—but if you lined up the Confederates along Route 3 at the end of the driveway you just followed, the line would stretch east almost to the visitor center.

It's also tough to imagine the difficulty of the terrain they had to traverse. The open fields today do let you see how uneven the rolling ground is, but you have to add to that the thick foliage the soldiers had to push through. Doing that shoulder to shoulder, with your rifle out in front of you, was even tougher. A number of small streams, hardly enough to make the ground soggy, also crisscross the area; on your way down the driveway, you crossed one such wet spot.

To the west, you can see a clearly defined hillcrest where Federal units in von Gilsa's Eleventh Corps division positioned themselves to face a possible flanking attack. While it's a strong position, it's not very big—and the number of Union units stationed there and facing west were easily overwhelmed by the advancing Confederate wave.

As you head back east on Route 3, you'll follow the same route the Confederates followed as they drove the Federal army back on its heels. One of the myths of Chancellorsville is that the Eleventh Corps completely broke and ran, but that's not entirely true. That perception came about because, as one historian noted, for each story of resistance and controlled withdrawal, "there was another story—or two or three stories—of utter demoralization and uncontrollable panic."

Another reason the Eleventh Corps was so maligned had much to do with xenophobia within the Union Army itself. Many of the units in the Eleventh Corps were composed of recently emigrated Germans—many so new to America that they spoke only a smattering of English. Even on their best days, the Germans of the Eleventh Corps faced discrimination and derision from soldiers in other parts of the army. On May 2, when the Eleventh Corps collapsed under the pressure of Jackson's onslaught, many non-German soldiers assumed the "flying Dutchmen" had turned tail and run simply because they were German.

Howard, for his part, admitted later that, "I wanted to die" because of the disaster that had befallen his corps. He lost some 2,400 men out of his total force of about eleven thousand—just under a quarter of his forces. One thousand of

The Union Eleventh Corps anchored itself on the knoll just beyond the two trees in the right side of the photo. The line then stretched along the crest of a ridge that ran to the left. There, it met the Orange Turnpike and curved eastward to run parallel to the road.

The Wilderness Church today.

them, caught off-guard by the suddenness of the attack, had been taken prisoner. In comparison, Jackson lost about eight hundred men.

As you travel to the next stop, 0.9 miles on the left, you'll pass the Wilderness Church. Originally built circa 1853 under the supervision of the Reverend Melzi S. Chancellor for his Baptist congregation, the wooden church stood two-and-a-half stories tall. "Little Wilderness Church...looks deserted and out of place," said a Union soldier who camped nearby on May 2. "Little did its worshippers on last sabbath day imagine what a conflict would rage about its walls before they again could meet within its peaceful precincts." The current church dates from 1899.

You'll also pass, about 1.1 miles from here on the right, a crescent-shaped monument for the 154th New York Infantry. When Colonel Adolphus Bushbeck tried to set up the second line of defense, some five thousand men rallied to his call. The 154th New York served as the centerpiece for that rally. The regiment's monument, dedicated in 1996, gets its shape from the insignia of the Eleventh Corps.

Beyond the 154th's monument on the right, 1.8 miles down the road, you'll see a private resort. That's the location

A monument marks the
approximate location of the
"Bushbeck Line," anchored by
the 154th New York Infantry,
which briefly stalled the
advance of Jackson's men.

where, as told in the prologue, the 8th Pennsylvania Cavalry
suddenly found itself trapped and had to fight its way to safety.

▶▶ **TO STOP 11:**

*From Stop 10, turn right onto Route 3 west. Get into the left lane.
Travel 0.3 miles, where you'll see a turning lane on the left. Use the
turning lane to reverse direction, using caution when you pull onto
Route 3 east. Travel 2 miles. As you near the turn for the Chancel-
lorsville Battlefield Visitor Center, you will take a right turn onto
Stuart Drive. Follow Stuart Drive 0.4 miles to Hazel Grove.
Pull over in the parking area on the right side of the road.*

CHAPTER ELEVEN

THE KEY TO THE BATTLEFIELD

Union Third Corps commander
Major General Dan Sickles,
feeling out of the action, chose
to launch a night attack,
which soon met with grief in
the dark woods.

The Wilderness played no favorites in its ability to bedevil the two armies. Even as Stonewall Jackson, trying to coordinate a night attack, was coming to personal grief along the Mountain Road, a mile to the south, Dan Sickles was plotting a night attack of his own.

The Third Corps commander's aggressiveness that afternoon had put him in an exposed position near Catharine Furnace, and the onset of darkness made him realize how vulnerable he was. By nine p.m., he carefully withdrew his men northward again to the high ground of Hazel Grove. Not content to simply wait out the night and see what the morning would bring, Sickles wanted to drive northward toward the Orange Turnpike and see if he could catch any Confederates in the dark.

What Sickles found instead, said one officer, was "a fine description of Pandemonium."

As his men advanced northward from Hazel Grove, many lost their bearings in the woods. Nervous soldiers soon started shooting at shadows, and the shadows shot back. Confederates started shooting, too. Federal artillery at the Chancellor house soon opened on the melee. Sickles' men attempted to escape the fusillade but then blundered into soldiers from the Union Twelfth Corps under Major General Henry Slocum. Although the Twelfth Corps had been warned to expect friendly soldiers moving across their front, they returned fire when Sickles' men fired on them first.

Union soldiers found themselves entangled in the dark Wilderness, unsure whether they faced friend or foe.

ON THE CONFEDERATE SIDE, JEB STUART WAS TRYING TO FIGURE OUT HOW TO RUN AN INFANTRY CORPS.

Sickles finally managed to pull his men back, and the pandemonium ceased. Nearly two hundred casualties resulted, mostly from friendly fire. "Whoever took part in the fizzle in the woods…" wrote one soldier, "will remember it as long as they live."

The Third Corps hunkered down on Hazel Grove to wait for morning after all.

★ ★ ★ ★ ★

On the Confederate side, Jeb Stuart was trying to figure out how to run an infantry corps. He'd commanded infantry only once before, in 1861, and on a far smaller scale. Now, he suddenly found himself in command of the entire Second Corps of the Army of Northern Virginia.

A.P. Hill, who had assumed command of the corps following Jackson's wounding, took a shell fragment across the backs of both of his legs moments after Jackson had been evacuated from the field. Hill sent word to Stuart, the only

major general left with the corps, to take over because the corps's other two division commanders—Rodes and Colston—were far too inexperienced.

Stuart got word of his new assignment at around midnight while leading a hit-and-run mission at Ely's Ford. He quickly wheeled around and headed to the front line.

In the meantime, the flank attack had come to a standstill. Stuart, when he arrived on the scene, chose not to jump-start things. He let the men of the Second Corps rest while he sent word to Jackson, asking if the wounded general had any instructions. Too weakened by his ordeal, Jackson could only reply, "Tell General Stuart he must do what he thinks best."

Stuart agreed to "press the pursuit already so gloriously begun," but in truth, he found himself in a highly vulnerable position. The flank attack had been a tremendous success, but now with momentum gone, the situation was far more precarious. The Confederate army was divided, with the bulk of the Federal army sitting between the two halves.

Lee, at his headquarters, immediately recognized the peril of his army and drafted orders for Stuart to do everything

After Jackson was accidentally wounded, his men carried him from the field as senior division commander A. P. Hill took charge. But soon thereafter, Hill fell wounded, too, and the Confederate attack remained stalled for the rest of the night.

Confederate artillerist Colonel Edward Porter Alexander.

possible to reunite the wings of the army, offering assurances that he would do the same. "It is necessary that the glorious victory thus far achieved be prosecuted with the utmost vigor, and the enemy given no time to rally," Lee added.

Stuart, showing Jackson-like resolve coupled with his own trademark flair, "never seemed to hesitate or to doubt for one moment that he could just crash his way wherever he chose to strike," a Confederate officer said.

Stuart began his preparations. The crashing would start at dawn.

* * * * *

Even as Stuart made his preparations to launch the Second Corps against the Federal position, Union commander Joe Hooker paid a predawn visit to Dan Sickles at Hazel Grove.

Hazel Grove, Hooker explained to Sickles, formed a salient in the Union line—an exposed position that jutted outward in a way that made it vulnerable to attack from multiple sides at once. With Lee's army positioned on either side of the salient, Sickles could expect irresistible pressure, Hooker believed.

Sickles disagreed. Hazel Grove was the best high ground in the area, and Sickles was certain he could defend it.

Hooker remained unconvinced. If anything went awry, the Third Corps would be cut off. He had already suffered one debacle with the Eleventh Corps; wanting to prevent another, he ordered Sickles to withdraw to a newly established line at Fairview, closer to the Chancellor house. The new line would be more defensible, Hooker maintained, and it would be closer to Hooker's reserves.

And so Sickles began his withdrawal, although the wet area around Lewis' Run caused a delay. That left the final elements of his artillery and infantry on Hazel Grove as daylight broke and Jeb Stuart gave the go-ahead for his morning assault.

Even as the last of Sickles' men withdrew from the hilltop, the lead elements of Stuart's attack appeared on the edge of

the clearing. "Fix bayonet!" their commander, Brigadier General James Archer, called. "Charge 'em, boys!" Confederate artillerist Porter Alexander set up a pair of batteries to support the charge. The Federals turned their orderly withdrawal into a hasty retreat, leaving behind three cannon and, more importantly, open access to Hazel Grove.

Like Jeb Stuart, Alexander had found himself thrust into command the previous night, replacing the Second Corps' wounded chief artillerist, Stapleton Crutchfield. Alexander knew nothing about the ground, the artillery positions, or the location of the Union batteries. He had spent the night giving himself a crash course on the tactical situation.

And now Joe Hooker had just given him the best artillery spot on the battlefield.

Alexander had his guns close at hand and ready to go: twenty-eight cannon in all, including the three just captured from Sickles' retreating artillerymen. He also ordered another fourteen guns up along the Plank Road to create converging fire on the new Federal position. "It was done very quickly," Alexander wrote.

He had to move with speed. Just over half a mile away in Fairview, the Federals were lining up guns of their own.

Even as Confederates moved artillery into position at Hazel Grove, Alexander sent other artillery pieces farther down the Orange Turnpike toward Fairview to set up enfilading fire.

TOUR STOP Hazel Grove

Once Confederate artillery took position on Hazel Grove, it began to pound Union positions at Fairview and Chancellorsville.

IT'S DIFFICULT TODAY TO GET A SENSE OF JUST HOW IDEAL the hilltop at Hazel Grove was as an artillery platform. In the seventy-square-mile sea of trees that made up the Wilderness, there were few open plots of ground, making the Wilderness a terrible place to deploy artillery. Open ground like Hazel Grove—which, in 1863, was entirely cleared of trees—was invaluable.

Hazel Grove was also ideal because of its elevation. Being on higher ground increases a gun's range while also making the gun harder to hit with counter-battery fire. Compared to Fairview two-thirds of a mile to the northeast, Hazel Grove does not have a particular advantage in elevation, but compared to the ground around the Chancellorsville intersection, it does. That's what made this position so important for the Confederates. The viewshed today provides a glimpse of the wide-open alley of fire toward the intersection that the Confederates enjoyed.

The artillery pieces you see on the hill represent only a small fraction of the Confederate guns posted here on the

morning of May 3. Two of the pieces are twelve-pounder Napoleons, originally designed for French Emperor Napoleon III. Napoleons became the most common artillery piece favored by both armies because they were relatively light to transport, yet they had a maximum range of up to seventeen hundred yards. Napoleons fired a twelve-pound solid shot (which is where the term "twelve-pounder" comes from), explosive shell, case shot, or canister.

Several cannons sit at Hazel Grove today.

Also on display is a "False Napoleon," a six-pounder gun "remodeled" after the war to resemble a twelve-pounder Napoleon. This was a relatively common practice used in the early days of battlefield commemoration. Historians typically used False Napoleons to stand in for real ones in places where there weren't enough actual Napoleons to go around.

The fourth gun on display is a twelve-pounder field howitzer. Howitzers fired rounds along a trajectory that arced higher, but went less distance, than a regular cannon. They were ideal for shooting over obstructions like breastworks.

Hazel Grove, at the time of the battle, was a bit more open than it is today. A farm occupied the site.

Union gunners had set up on this position on April 30, and on May 1, they fired on Confederates trying to work their way around the right flank of the Union army. The same artillerists also opened fire on Stonewall Jackson's column as it undertook its flank march on May 2 (the gap in the trees visible at Stop 6, which revealed the column's position to the Union gunners, is no longer visible because the forest is now older and taller).

At the time of the battle, a one-and-a-half story wooden building sat at Hazel Grove. Built between 1837 and 1838 by Melzi Chancellor, who lived at Dowdall's Tavern to the west, the building may have served as a home for one or all seven of the slaves Chancellor owned. Several dependencies, including a spring house and a log stable or barn, also sat on the site, as did a small orchard beyond the crest of the hill.

When Confederates launched the flank attack, the buildings at Hazel Grove served as hospitals. "[T]here was an old stable, into which many of the wounded had been carried, and from which throughout the night commingled moans and groans of the wounded and dying," wrote a soldier from the 12th New Hampshire. "The piteous, heart-piercing cries of one poor fellow, continuing until the angel of death heard and

Gunners at Hazel Grove had a clear avenue of fire in the direction of Fairview.

A monument to Confederate Brigadier General Frank Paxton sits on the road to Hazel Grove, just past the turn from Route 3.

came to his relief...." The barn survived the battle, as did the spring house, but the main house did not. By early on May 3, fighting had destroyed it.

Between 1866-68, the remains of seventy-five Union soldiers buried between this vicinity were disinterred and moved to the National Cemetery in Fredericksburg.

Today, the Hazel Grove clearing is smaller than it was in 1863. To the west, the treeline hides modern development.

▶▶ **TO STOP 12:**

From Stop 11, drive 0.1 mile and turn left onto Berry–Paxton Drive. Follow Berry–Paxton Drive to the end and park.

CHAPTER TWELVE
THE CRUCIBLE OF BATTLE

Union gunners at Fairview had an open field of fire on the Confederate artillery on Hazel Grove. Their biggest problem wouldn't be the Confederates—it would be keeping their own guns supplied with enough ammunition to continue the terrible duel.

Even as James Archer's brigade swept onto the crest of the recently abandoned Hazel Grove, the rest of the Confederate Second Corps surged forward. Confederate brigades swept southeasterly through the woods while others drove straight down the Plank Road. James Lane's brigade, including the 18th North Carolina, was at the forefront of the fray. "Remember Jackson!" some of them cried, while others let loose the Rebel Yell.

Waiting to meet the Confederates were elements of the Union Third and Twelfth Corps, some of them tucked behind low breastworks they had constructed during the night. The Confederates swept into the Union line and, according to one Union soldier, "a long, fierce, and desperate contest" ensued. There was, he said, "no stopping, no breathing space...."

Major General Hiram Berry, a native of Maine who commanded a division in the Third Corps, was shot as he crossed the Plank Road. "I am dying," he told his staff when they came to his aid. "Carry me to the rear." By the time they reached the Chancellor house, Berry was dead. Hooker, when he saw Berry's body, was taken aback. "My God, Berry, why did this have to happen?" Hooker exclaimed. "Why does the man I relied on so have to be taken away in this manner?"

As the terrible back-and-forth continued, Captain Clermont Best put his forty-four guns into action at Fairview. He had only a slight advantage in numbers over the Confederate artillery, but several disadvantages weighed against him.

Private Rice Bull of the 123rd New York Infantry.

Confederate Brigadier General Elisha F. "Frank" Paxton, commander of the Stonewall Brigade.

The first was "converging fire"—Confederates from multiple positions concentrated their artillery on his single position.

Complicating matters, Best had to fire over the heads of his own men—never an ideal option since it was tremendously demoralizing, not to mention devastating whenever a shell accidentally burst prematurely and killed members of the artillerists' own army. "The noise was deafening as the shells went howling and singing over our heads, and we nervously ducked as they went by," wrote Rice Bull of the 123rd New York Infantry. Bull's regiment was locked in struggle with some of Lane's North Carolinians.

As Stuart fed fresh troops into the fight, Hooker ordered a counterattack. Men under Major General William French swept out of their entrenchments in a northwesterly direction, pushing back the disorganized Confederate hordes that had gained so much hard-fought ground that morning. "The rebels ran like a plague had fallen among them," a Union officer wrote.

The attack bogged down just north of the Plank Road. "The country is the worst possible for aggressive warfare," one soldier complained. "It is heavily wooded & is very broken. We cannot see a hundred yards in front of us." Another soldier saw that terrain as an advantage. "I presume the thick woods protected us," he wrote, "as nearly every tree had a ball in it."

To the south of the Plank Road, a back-and-forth struggle continued. Union and Confederate soldiers charged and countercharged between two sets of earthworks. The colonel of the 18th North Carolina suffered a mortal wound, their lieutenant colonel was knocked out of action, and their color-bearer, who was killed, lost the regimental colors.

In another charge, members of the Stonewall Brigade claimed they would show their fellow Confederates "how to clear away a Federal line." Their commander, Frank Paxton, a hometown friend of Stonewall Jackson's from Lexington, Virginia, was shot through the heart as he led the advance. The brigade shortly thereafter fell back, having failed to clear the Federals.

The cannonade from Fairfield also continued to have its effect. The 10th Virginia Infantry, attacking north of the Plank Road, lost a colonel and a major to the artillery fire coming from the south of them. "I was shot in the foot," wrote one of the regiment's captains, "and in 15 minutes after I was shot through the hip, which near disabled me." The tide of battle swept past him and he prepared to surrender, but then it swept back in the other direction, giving him the chance to make an escape. He was hit then a third time but managed to "exit from the field by the assistance of a friend."

"Carnage is fearful," telegraphed a Union officer. And it was only 8:30 in the morning.

Stuart threw in his last line, the division of Robert Rodes, at around 9:00 a.m. The push was enough to finally dislodge the Union army from its breastworks south of the Plank Road, which suddenly put the Confederates in a position to threaten the Union artillery position at Fairview. It was a costly push, though: Brigadier General Stephen Ramseur's brigade, which led the final assault, successfully led the punch through the Federal line but, in doing so, lost more than half of its strength, and one regiment, the 4th North Carolina, suffered a casualty rate of nearly 80 percent. Ramseur, seeing the carnage that befell his men, "wept like a child."

Confederates kept exerting pressure on the Union position, but Union soldiers resisted, exacting terrible casualties. It would become the bloodiest morning of the war.

Confederate Brigadier General Stephen Dodson Ramseur.

The Wilderness was hardly less confusing in the daylight than it had been the previous evening. The close-quarters fighting turned into a brutal slugfest. The dense foliage made it difficult to maneuver.

Union Major General Hiram Berry.

According to one Georgian, the Fairfield artillerists "threw grape, canister bombs, balls, and nearly everything else" at the Confederates now threatening their position. That firepower kept the Confederates at bay—for the moment.

To the southeast, Robert E. Lee ordered the divisions of Anderson and McLaws to begin attacking. Anderson's division put pressure on Fairfield from a new direction, making the position even more difficult to maintain. A series of charges and countercharges turned the field into chaos. Every time the Confederate infantry would pull back, said one Union soldier, Confederate artillerists on Hazel Grove "poured the shells over into us in perfect showers."

But that wasn't all. As more Confederate batteries rolled into position on Hazel Grove, some of them began to take aim at Joseph Hooker himself.

Fairview

Today, several artillery lunettes remain at Fairview, showing the original Union line facing due west and then the resituated line of May 3 facing toward Hazel Grove, visible in the distance.

IN THE OPEN FIELDS SURROUNDING FAIRVIEW ARE LOW, criss-crossing mounds of earth called lunettes (the word means "half-moon," which describes their shape). These lunettes surrounded and protected some of the thirty-four artillery pieces that dominated Fairview heights. Today they remain as silent witnesses to the battle. We ask visitors to please refrain from walking on them or on other fortifications.

The Union artillerymen who dug these lunettes initially faced their line to the south. As the battle raged and Jackson launched his flank attack, many of the artillery pieces were turned to face to the west; the lunettes were re-dug to face west as well.

Union soldiers tried to fortify their contracted line by digging earthworks, seen here after the war.

Looking southwest, the guns atop these heights had a good field of fire toward Hazel Grove, where thirty Confederate cannon were perched. The narrow vista between the two farms witnessed heavy artillery fire along with some of the bloodiest infantry fighting of the war.

Fairview, which appeared in many soldier letters as "the frame house," "the log cabin," and "the overseers house," was a one-and-a-half story log cabin built circa 1809. Owned by

Fairview, across from Chancellorsville, was a successful farm prior to the war.

James Moxley, overseer of the plantation at Fairview, lived with his family in a log cabin at this spot.

Ann and Richard Pound, the building originally served as a tavern and inn. The adjacent land also had a cemetery, a well, an orchard, and at least one outbuilding. Following Richard's death, Ann remarried, and in 1816 she and her new husband, George Chancellor, moved into a new home on the other side of the road, closer to the intersection.

By the time of the war, the log cabin at Fairview was occupied by James and Roberta Moxley and their children. Moxley was the overseer of the Chancellorsville plantation, with twenty slaves under his charge. When the Union army marched into the area on April 29, the Moxleys fled, first to Catharine Furnace, then beyond. The slaves vanished from historical record.

The building sustained a few scars during the battle, but it remained standing and sturdy enough to be used as a field hospital after the fight. "The old log cabin was…the center of our colony and around it [were] more than five hundred wounded men," wrote one of the patients. "In it were placed those thought to be most dangerously wounded and most needing surgical treatment. One man…was wildly deliri-

ous…. His end came at night, and was tragic….he jumped up and ran and entered the cabin through the front door. On the further side of the room was a large dish shelf about three feet above the floor on which was a lighted candle. The demented man must have seen the light, and started for it, trampling on the wounded men on the way. He laid down on the shelf and died before morning."

Although the log cabin was destroyed later in the month, remnants of its stone chimneys still exist. The old well, now capped, is also visible. A low brick wall hems in the Chancellor family cemetery. Twenty-eight monuments mark the graves of various family members, although several individuals are buried in the cemetery without markers. The oldest marker belongs to George Chancellor (1785-1836), the family patriarch. His wife, Ann (1793-1860), was the widow of Captain Richard Pound, the original owner of Fairview who is interred in the cemetery in one of the unmarked graves. The youngest person resting in the cemetery is Susie E. Guy (1863-1866), who died on her third birthday, Sept. 29. The last Chancellor buried in the cemetery was Susan Margaret

Following the battle, Fairview became a field hospital for wounded soldiers of both sides.

HERE ARE INTERRED

GEORGE CHANCELLOR, ESQUIRE (1785 – 1836)
OF CHANCELLORSVILLE
SON OF JOHN AND ELIZABETH (EDWARDS) CHANCELLOR AND
GRANDSON OF JOHN CHANCELLOR (1726 – 1815) AND HIS WIFE
NÉE JANE MONROE, AUNT OF PRESIDENT JAMES MONROE.
IN 1814 HE MARRIED
ANN (LYON) POUND (1783 – 1860)
ONLY DAUGHTER OF JAMES LYON (1755 – 1836) OF FALMOUTH, VA.
AND HIS WIFE NÉE MARY LONGWILL (1748 – 1794) OF CECIL CO. MD.
ANN WAS THE WIDOW OF CAPTAIN RICHARD POUND OF FAIRVIEW WHO
IS ALSO INTERRED HERE. AS A WEDDING GIFT HER ONLY HALF
BROTHER, WILLIAM LORMAN, ESQ. (1764 – 1841) OF BALTIMORE,
ERECTED THE MANSION CALLED CHANCELLORSVILLE IN 1815 – 1816.

CHANCELLOR

The Chancellor family cemetery still remains at Fairview.

Chancellor (1847-1935). Several of the men interred in the cemetery served with the Confederate army, and at least two of them died during the war.

On your way to Stop 12, as you head back down Berry-Paxton Drive, you'll pass the 27th Indiana Infantry regimental marker about one-tenth of a mile on your right. It's one of the few monuments on the entire battlefield. The 27th Indiana is best known as the unit that found Robert E. Lee's "Lost Order"—Special Order 191—outside Frederick, Maryland, which outlined Lee's plans for the Confederate invasion of Maryland in the fall of 1862.

At Chancellorsville, the 27th Indiana escaped the worst of the fighting on May 2, even absorbing some soldiers from regiments manhandled by Jackson's attack. When Confederates resumed their attacks on the morning of May 3, in their effort to reunite the two wings of their army, things got hot for the Indianans. Colonel Silas Colgrove, operating a pair of abandoned cannon he'd pressed into service, shouted to his son, the regiment's major, "Here, boy, you run the regiment while I run this here gun." The 27th Indiana, along with the rest of its brigade, repulsed several Confederate charges from the direction of Hazel Grove, withdrawing only because the entire Union position was collapsing.

On your way to Stop 12, you will drive down Slocum Drive. As you do, you'll pass a pull-off for Slocum's Line. If you stop, you'll see earthworks on the right side of the road. This line of earthworks marks the position of the Twelfth Corps on the morning of May 3, just before Confederates in Anderson's division began to attack.

As you'll remember from Stop 11, Slocum's Twelfth Corps saw some strange things on the night of May 2. When Dan Sickles' men got lost in the woods as they tried to make their night attack, some of them brushed into men of the Twelfth Corps stationed along part of this line. Several hours later, when James Archer's Confederates swept over Hazel Grove, they followed the retreating Federals in this direction but ran into the Twelfth Corps. After a brief fight, Slocum's men forced the Confederates to withdraw.

The monument for the 27th Indiana Infantry is one of the few regimental monuments on the Chancellorsville battlefield.

TO STOP 13:

▶▶ *From the parking area, follow Berry-Paxton Drive back to the stop sign. Turn left and go 0.1 of a mile. At the "Y" at the top of the hill, bear to the left. This will put you on Slocum Drive, which is a one-way road. Follow Slocum Drive 0.6 miles until it intersects with Old Plank Road. Take a left on Old Plank Road and follow it 0.2 miles until you come to the traffic light. Go straight through the light. On the left, you'll see a parking area at the former site of the Chancellorsville Inn.*

Union Colonel Silas Colgrove of the 27th Indiana.

CHAPTER THIRTEEN

"AGONY AND CONFLICT"

———•———

By midmorning on May 3, battle enveloped the Chancellorsville crossroads.

Days earlier, Joe Hooker had proclaimed that his plans were perfect. Now, as he stood on the front porch of the Chancellor house on the morning of May 3, those perfect plans were unraveling before his eyes.

He'd spent much of the morning riding his lines, urging on his men, keeping up their spirits, showing everyone why he'd earned the nickname "Fighting Joe." Union soldiers responded with grim enthusiasm, matching charge with countercharge and going toe-to-toe with the Confederate army in what would become the bloodiest morning of the entire war and the second-bloodiest single day second only to Antietam. "[B]ullets…fell like rain drops in a summer shower," one soldier wrote.

Withdrawing the Third Corps from Hazel Grove and into a tighter defensive position had, Hooker thought, been a sound military decision. "The position I abandoned was one that I had held at a disadvantage," he would say, after the war, as way of explanation.

But from the front porch, as Hooker watched Confederate artillery perched on Hazel Grove trade blows with his own artillery at Fairview and in the clearing around the Chancellor house, he began to realize the tide of battle had begun to shift against him. Confederate artillery that would never have otherwise come into play because of the thick woods had a perfect platform from which to bombard the Union position.

Hooker tried to reassure his men that the injury he suffered had not debilitated him or knocked him out of action, although shortly after waving to his men from horseback he was struck by a spell of wooziness and had to be helped from his horse.

Hooker sent word to John Sedgwick, still in Fredericksburg, urging the Sixth Corps commander to move with all possible haste to Hooker's assistance. Unbeknownst to Hooker, Sedgwick first had to storm Marye's Heights, where Confederates were hunkered down behind the same stone wall that had caused the Union army so much grief the previous December during the Battle of Fredericksburg. Once through the Confederate position, Sedgwick would be able to move down the Orange Turnpike and come upon a portion of Lee's army from the rear.

A courier rode up to Hooker with a dispatch. Just as the general reached for it, a Confederate shell screamed toward them and slammed into the wooden column next to Hooker, sending splinters everywhere. A huge chuck of the column smashed into the general, knocking him to the porch floor, senseless.

Witnesses thought Hooker was dead. He lay unconscious for more than half an hour, and even after he revived, he was insensible. At one point, he tried to mount his horse so he could show his troops he was okay, but the attempt made him sick. Hooker's doctor convinced the general to lie down on a blanket, and eventually, he evacuated the general to the rear, to a position near the Bullock Farm. A few moments after Hooker left, a Confederate shell struck the blanket where the commander had been resting.

"For the remainder of the day he was wandering, and was unable to get any ideas into his head," wrote a member of Hooker's staff. The doctor declared that Hooker had a severe concussion. He "suffered great pain and was in a comatose condition for most of the time," said a Union general. "His mind was not clear, and they had to wake him up to communicate with him."

Despite his injury, Hooker refused to turn over command. And so, for nearly an hour—as the tide shifted against the Union army, as Stuart and Lee reunited their forces and attacked all along the line, as Union guns withdrew from Fairview because they'd run out of ammunition—the Army of the Potomac suffered from a lack of leadership.

* * * * *

Hooker's head wound incapacitated him for more than an hour and forced him to withdraw from the Chancellor House. He fell back a mile to the site of the Bullock House (above) and there established a new headquarters. The army soon fell back, as well.

The Federal Second Corps held open the lines of retreat for the Union army, which gave up ground only grudgingly.

As the Union position at Fairview collapsed, Porter Alexander moved several of his artillery pieces forward from Hazel Grove to take up position where the Federal guns had been just moments earlier. "We deployed on the plateau, & opened on the fugitives, infantry, artillery, wagons—everything—swarming about the Chancellorsville house, & down the broad road leading thence to the river," Porter later wrote.

During the barrage, the Chancellor house caught fire. Members of the Chancellor family and several neighbors, all huddled in the basement, were told by a member of Hooker's staff that they had to flee. Sixteen fugitives bolted from the house, through the roar of battle, to find safety. "The woods around the house were a sheet of fire—the air filled with shot and shell—horses were running, rearing and screaming—the men, a mass of confusion, moaning, cursing, and praying," recalled one of the refugees. Hooker's staff member took them up the road that led first to the Bullock Farm and then beyond to U.S. Ford, where a chaplain then escorted them across the Rappahannock.

Although the Confederates had driven the Union army back from the Chancellorsville intersection, two fresh Federal Corps—the First and Fifth—remained ready for battle. Hooker based his new line on the strength of the two corps.

Major General Darius Couch, commander of the Second Corps, led the final defense of the Chancellorsville intersection as the Union army tried to extract itself from the calamity that had befallen it. The Federals fought stubbornly even as they fell back to a new line established by George Gordon Meade's Fifth Corps, with its apex across the road from the Bullock Farm. Meade had urged Hooker to let him wade into the fray with his fresh corps as well as with the fresh First Corps—nearly thirty thousand troops in all—but Hooker had held them back as insurance to stay any possible rout that might occur. The First and Fifth Corps were Hooker's last line of defense.

Lee, seeing that the Chancellorsville intersection now belonged in Confederate hands, rode down from Hazel Grove. When he arrived at the clearing around the house, his men parted to let him pass. "One long, unbroken cheer, in which the feeble cry of those who lay helpless on the earth blended with the strong voices of those who still fought, rose high above the roar of battle, and hailed the presence of the victorious chief," wrote one of Lee's aides-de-camp.

Sitting atop his white horse, Traveller, with the Chancellor mansion engulfed in flames behind him, Lee removed his hat and acknowledged his men. "He sat," wrote Lee's staffer, "in the full realization of all that soldiers dream of—triumph."

Union Major General Darius Couch, the Federal army's ranking corps commander, could have taken over for the wounded Hooker, but Hooker refused to relinquish command even though he was obviously incapacitated.

TOUR STOP Chancellorsville

Although the Chancellor House burned down during the battle, it was later rebuilt. All that remains today, though, is the outline of the house's foundation.

WHEN THE BATTLE OF CHANCELLORSVILLE OPENED, THE Chancellor family, along with ten other refugees, hid in the basement of the house. "Up-stairs they were bringing in the wounded and we could hear their screams of pain," Sue recalled. "They had taken our sitting room as an operating room, and our piano served as an amputating table." Outside the window, doctors had heaped a large pile of limbs they had amputated from their patients and "rows and rows of dead bodies covered with canvas" had been lined up nearby.

When Confederate shells set the Chancellor home on fire, and the refugees fled from the basement, Sue would forever remember the last look she had of her "old home…completely enveloped in flames." The Union officer that led them to safety, Colonel Joseph Dickinson, faced some criticism for his effort, but he would not forsake the civilians. "If here is not the post of duty, looking after the safety of these helpless

women and children," he told one officer who challenged him, "then I don't know what you call duty."

Sue Chancellor wrote her account of the battle seventy-two years later in 1935. "[T]he years have dimmed my memory as to incidents and occurrences," she admitted, "yet the horrible impression of those days of agony and conflict is still vivid and I can close my eyes and see again the blazing woods, the house in flames, the flying shot and shell, and the terror stricken women and children pushing their way over the dead and wounded, led by the courageous and chivalrous [Colonel] Dickinson."

When Lee arrived at the Chancellorsville intersection, his men erupted in "one long, unbroken cheer."

"BEYOND THE CROSSROADS"

Salem Church today.

To the east, John Sedgwick broke through the Confederate line and, as Hooker had ordered, drove westward. Lee caught wind of Sedgwick's movements, though, and sent a force out to intercept him along a ridgeline next to Old Salem Church. Surprised to find more resistance, Sedgwick tried to fight his way through but ended up withdrawing into a defensive position around Banks' Ford.

And so, May 4 passed with Sedgwick pinned up around the ford and Hooker hunkered down behind his last line. Lee looked for a way to strike, but neither situation offered a clear opportunity, and so the day passed—as did any chance Lee had for destroying the Federal army in detail.

At a council of war that night, several of Hooker's subordinates argued in favor of launching an offensive or at least staying in position and inviting Lee to attack, but Hooker overruled them and withdrew both sections of the Federal army back across the Rappahannock. "[T]he men were absolutely astonished at our move," said a Wisconsin officer, "for everyone felt that we had the best of the rebs and could hold our position…till hell froze over."

In its wake, the Union army left behind about thirteen percent of its men—some seventeen thousand killed, wounded, or missing. "My God! My God!" exclaimed President Lincoln when he heard the news. "What will the country say?"

As the Union army retreated and the Confederate army advanced, they passed over a landscape strewn with casualties from both sides.

"Fighting Joe" had the fight knocked out of him at Chancellorsville. He would spend the rest of the war trying to repair his damaged reputation.

Soldiers in the Union army, dispirited, felt more like they'd been cheated rather than defeated. "We marched, we fought, we failed," wrote one Indiana soldier. "We were not defeated but we did not defeat."

Blame came to rest squarely on Hooker's shoulders. Brigadier General Alpheus Williams summed up the army's—and the public's—feelings pretty well: "We have lost physically and numerically, but still more morally… by universal want of confidence in the commanding officer."

Hooker would retain command of the army until late June, when the mounting frustrations between him and his commander-in-chief finally led to Hooker's removal. Major General George Gordon Meade would replace him, just days before the two armies clashed in the crossroads town of Gettysburg.

Compared to their northern counterparts, the Confederate army lost twenty-two percent of its men, totaling nearly thirteen thousand killed, wounded, and missing. The most grievous loss for the Confederates was Stonewall Jackson, who died on Sunday, May 10 at 3:15 in the afternoon. "I know not how to replace him," Lee later said.

Although the war continued for two more years, the Battle of Chancellorsville represented a kind of high water mark for the Confederacy: The Army of Northern Virginia never again won a decisive battlefield victory.

As the Federal army retreated, many Union soldiers felt discouraged by the army's performance. "We were not defeated but we did not defeat," one of them wrote.

THE RIVERS AND FORDS

Germanna Ford today.

Meandering through the Wilderness of Spotsylvania, Orange, and Culpepper Counties are two natural barriers, the Rapidan and Rappahannock Rivers. During the war, the rivers saw men march off to battle, heads held high; they saw many of those same men take refuge along their banks, broken and battered but not defeated.

Yet even before the war, the two rivers were important features of the Wilderness.

The shallow Rapidan River emerges from Virginia's Shenandoah Valley and flows eastward until it reaches the Rappahannock River northwest of the city of Fredericksburg. One of the earliest settlements along the river, Germanna, was located near where modern day Route 3 crosses the river into Culpepper County.

The ford at Germanna became a major crossing point for the Union and Confederate armies throughout the Civil War. In particular, it was a key route for movement during the Chancellorsville Campaign as well as the Wilderness Campaign of 1864.

Larger than the Rapidan, the Rappahannock also boasted many important crossings: Ely's Ford, Banks' Ford, and United States Ford, as well as lesser fords. On the river's shore sat the strategically placed city of Fredericksburg. Deep-water ships could navigate to the city to pick up goods brought in from the Virginia piedmont. From Fredericksburg, steamers could then follow the river southeast into the Chesapeake

The 8th Pennsylvania Cavalry, which would find itself trapped between the Confederate skirmish line and battle line on May 2, arrived at Chancellorsville via Ely's Ford.

Bay, where they could then turn north and head to Fredericksburg's sister city, Baltimore, Maryland.

Throughout the winter of 1862-63, Confederate pickets had outposts at many of the Rappahannock's crossing points. Union engineers, meanwhile, spent the winter scouting the sites, taking notes on the river's depth, the base material at each crossing, and whether artillery or wagons could be moved across at each point. Then, just prior to the start of the Chancellorsville Campaign, the Union army secured many of the fords to facilitate the army's sweeping flanking movement. Once across the rivers, the army needed the fords for transportation and communication.

Once the battle opened, Confederates failed in their attempts to cut the Union army off from the major crossings sites. This proved invaluable to the Federals, who eventually used the crossings to retreat to safety.

During the 1864 Campaign, the Union army's Second Corps crossed the Rappahannock at Ely's Ford while the rest

The following handwritten text appears on the sketch:

The 2nd to 3rd Corps crossing the pontoons at the United States ford. The crossing was effected by moonlight Thursday evening April 31st, 1863.

In the wood May 2nd. There is very little fighting going on today. Gen Hooker seems to be acting on the defensive for the purpose of drawing the enemy from his position. Moonlight

of the army crossed at Germanna. This time, Federal soldiers would never again retreat across the river in failure. The Union commander, Lieutenant General Ulysses S. Grant, drove south toward Richmond and never turned back.

Today many of the river crossings still exist, although some are on private property. However, Ely's Ford on Route 610 is a public boat launch. Visitors are encouraged to take the short drive north and visit the ford. From the Chancellorsville intersection, travel north on Route 610 for approximately six miles.

Notice how shallow the river is and look at the rocky base, which made crossing easier. To speed movements, the Union Army would lay temporary bridges, known as pontoon bridges, for artillery and supply wagons.

The steep banks demonstrate what formidable geographic barriers rivers in Virginia could be, which made fords all that much more important. Because the banks are so steep, please do be careful near the edges.

A sketch of Federal soldiers crossing at United States Ford on April 30.

MATTHEW FONTAINE MAURY

Matthew Fontaine Maury.

On many maps, it was simply labeled the "Brick House." Yet the two-story brick home that stood here, built between 1820-1821, had its own historic importance. It was built on the site where Matthew Fontaine Maury was born.

Despite coming from such a landlocked part of Virginia, Maury would eventually become known as the father of modern oceanography.

Maury was born in an unassuming house in 1806, but the family would spend little time in Spotsylvania County. By the time Maury was four, his family moved to Franklin, Tennessee.

Although Maury did not live near the ocean, it called to him. At the age of nineteen, he disobeyed his father's wishes and entered the United States Navy, eventually earning commission as a midshipman. One of his first assignments would be to accompany the hero Marquis de Lafayette back to France following Lafayette's post-war tour of the United States. Maury's seagoing days were cut short, though, at the age of thirty-three, when he was seriously injured in a stagecoach accident.

In 1842, Maury accepted the prestigious assignment as the first superintendent of the United States Naval Observatory. The post allowed him to study many aspects of the

A short trail leads from the parking lot to the ruins of the Maury House.

world's oceans, including meteorology and currents, and he learned the intricacies of modern naval equipment. Maury also pored over the charts and logbooks of ship captains, collecting as much information as possible on the world's oceans. This would open the seas for further exploration while also helping more ships navigate more safely.

Maury's work encompassed not only the world's oceans but also the world's land masses and even its meteorology. Foreign leaders were so impressed that they helped to fund his research even though the United States refused to.

Believing that the United States needed a school for sailors, Maury became an outspoken advocate for the creation of the United States Naval Academy at Annapolis, Maryland. When war erupted between the states, though, Maury chose to leave his successful career with the Navy to side with the Confederacy. He was, by some accounts, the world's most famous southerner to join the Confederate cause.

All that remains of the
Maury House today is a
small pile of bricks.

Although Maury did not see active service with the
Confederacy, he traveled abroad to secure ships and supplies
for the fledgling Confederate Navy. He also put his scientific
knowledge to work, inventing an electric torpedo, which, for
its time, was quite effective.

Following the war, Maury accepted a position to teach at
the Virginia Military Institute. He was also a driving force
behind the creation of the Virginia Agricultural and
Mechanical College—modern-day Virginia Tech.

While living in Lexington, Maury struck up a friendship
with the president of Washington College, Robert E. Lee.
When Lee died in 1870, Maury was asked to be a pallbearer.

Maury lived in Lexington until his own death on February 1,
1873. He was first buried in the Lexington City Cemetery,
but later his remains were exhumed and reburied in Hollywood
Cemetery in Richmond, overlooking the James River. A large
bronze statue honoring Maury's contributions to science sits
sentinel along Richmond's Monument Boulevard. Dedicated
on November 11, 1929, it was the last of the Civil War statues
placed along the famed boulevard.

in 1929, sits along Monument
Avenue in Richmond, Virginia.

Today there is little evidence of the original house, or
the "brick house." We encourage the visitor to walk out and
read the park interpretive signs—and get a feel for the
Wilderness, too.

OPPOSITE PAGE, TOP: On May 1, Union Major General George Sykes held a position that overlooked open fields of fire to the east, which Confederates would have had to cross.

OPPOSITE PAGE, BOTTOM: On May 2, Jackson's surprise attack slammed into the Union flank, positioned along the crest of this small hill.

BELOW: On May 3, Union artillery pulled out of Fairview after they began to run out of ammunition.

Union trenches snake through the Wilderness.

The Stonewall Jackson monument near the visitor center.

ABOUT THE AUTHOR

Chris Mackowski, an associate professor of journalism and mass communication at St. Bonaventure University, has won numerous awards for his writing. He is the co-author of *The Last Days of Stonewall Jackson* and the author of *The Dark, Close Wood: The Wilderness, Ellwood, and the Battle that Redefined Both*, as well as numerous Civil War articles. He works as a historical interpreter at Fredericksburg & Spotsylvania National Military Park.